D1118360

BISON
BOOKS

DATE DUE   OCT 18 '06

OCT	2 3 2009		

Demco, Inc. 38-293

OCLC record

INDIAN WAR IN THE
PACIFIC NORTHWEST

THE JOURNAL OF
LIEUTENANT LAWRENCE KIP

INTRODUCTION TO THE BISON BOOKS EDITION BY
CLIFFORD E. TRAFZER

UNIVERSITY OF NEBRASKA PRESS
LINCOLN AND LONDON

Introduction © 1999 by the University of Nebraska Press
Manufactured in the United States of America

∞

First Bison Books printing: 1999
Most recent printing indicated by the last digit below:
10   9   8   7   6   5   4   3   2   1

Library of Congress Cataloging-in-Publication Data
Kip, Lawrence, 1836–1899.
[Army life on the Pacific]
Indian War in the Pacific Northwest: the journal of Lieuten-
ant Lawrence Kip / introduction to the Bison Books edition
by Clifford E. Trafzer.
p. cm.
Originally published: Army life on the Pacific. New York:
Redfield, 1859. With new introd.
Includes bibliographical references and index.
ISBN 0-8032-7791-1 (pbk.: alk. paper)
1. Coeur d'Alene War, 1858—Personal narratives. 2. Kip,
Lawrence, 1836–1899. 3. United States. Army. Regiment of
Artillery, 3rd. I. Title.
E83.84.K57   1999
973.6′8—dc21
99-31674   CIP

This Bison Books edition follows the original in beginning
Chapter 1 on arabic page 9; no material has been omitted.

INTRODUCTION

Clifford E. Trafzer

In 1978, Lucy Covington, former tribal chair of the Colville Confederated Nation, gave a lecture on American Indian sovereignty at the Davenport Hotel in Spokane, Washington. She prefaced her presentation by saying that whenever she visited the city, her heart sank because of the deaths of Indians that occurred near Spokane during the Plateau Indian War of 1855. For Covington and many Plateau Indians, the events described in Lawrence Kip's *Indian War in the Pacific Northwest* are not something solely of the past but of the present. Kip's descriptions of the war are presented in this volume, and these events have affected the lives of American Indians from the Columbia Plateau since 1855. As Nez Perce elder Andrew George once said, historical events seem like they happened yesterday, appearing to people like dreams.[1] But these were real events that continue to influence the lives of contemporary native people.

Lawrence Kip was born in or near New York City on September 17, 1836, the son of William Ingraham Kip and Maria Elizabeth Lawrence. His father was an Episcopal priest who became the first bishop of California. In 1853 at the age of sixteen, Kip entered the United States Military Academy at West Point, studying as a cadet for a year before resigning to join his parents in California. When he turned eighteen, Kip joined the Third Artillery in Oregon to fight in the Rogue River War.[2] Kip continued his military service in the newly created Washington

Territory and in 1855 was stationed at Fort Dalles along the lower Columbia River. Kip was a product of his age, and his work demonstrates the dual nature of his country's approach to Native Americans. The concepts of Manifest Destiny and Mission are both found in this book, as Kip describes the aggressive war launched against Native Americans in the inland Northwest in 1858 and the non-violent treaty council held in the Walla Walla Valley three years before.[3]

Throughout the document, Kip's portrayals of whites and Indians reflect the national attitude of superiority over "savage" native nations and the supposed benevolence of his country to offer Indians a better way of life through three treaties. Kip's account is one of Manifest Destiny working against Native Americans who challenged federal authority by going to war to protect their people, culture, and "splendid country." The lieutenant admits that the soldiers "cannot wonder that" the Indians "are aroused when they think the white men are intruding on them." This was one of the few admissions that the Indians were reacting to an invasion of their country by white men bent on forcing their will and ways on native people. By 1855, Northwestern Indians had experienced a lengthy association with explorers, traders, trappers, and missionaries.[4] But the era between 1855, when Kip attended the Walla Walla Council, and 1858, when he participated in the final phase of the Plateau Indian War, was a watershed in Native American history—one that changed native life forever.

In 1853, the United States divided Oregon Territory into two territories, marking a dramatic change in Indian-white relations. In 1854 and 1855, Washington Territorial Governor Isaac Stevens and Oregon Superintendent of Indian Affairs Joel Palmer set out to bring American Indian policy to the various tribes of Oregon and Washington territories by negotiating treaties and establishing reservations where the United States concentrated as many Indians as possible. Through treaties, the United States "legally" liquidated Indian title to the land, while the tribes secured for themselves a minute portion of their former lands.[5] The negotiations, treaties, and reservations created by the agreements pushed the Indians into a defensive position. As Chief Kamiakin stated, after the Walla Walla Council numerous tribes took "common cause . . . to defend altogether our nationality and our country."[6]

Still, in May and June 1855, Kamiakin and his uncles, Owhi and Teias, as well as the leadership of the Nez Perces, Walla Wallas, Umatillas, and Cayuses met Stevens and Palmer at the council grounds. Kip's observations of the council provide his own impressions of the proceedings, including a colorful first-hand account of 2,500 Nez Perces riding single file into the council. Dressed in their finest clothing and colorfully painted, Nez Perces entered the council clashing their war shields and singing the same song—one that is still sung today. Kip reports that the Nez Perces called themselves "Chipunish," which they did not.[7] Then as now, the people call themselves *Nimipu*, the people.[8] Kip notes correctly that "a German soldier of Governor Stevens' party" made drawings of the council. This was Gustavus Sohon who left us our only graphic representations of the meeting.[9]

Kip's account of the Walla Walla Council does not mention the important meeting between Yakama-Palouse Chief Kamiakin and Governor Stevens on June 9, 1855, when Kamiakin told Stevens that he would not sign the treaty.[10] According to an account written by interpreter Andrew Pambrun, Stevens threatened Kamiakin, telling him to sign the agreement or face bloodshed.[11] Doty explains that there was a long pause and that Kamiakin finally consented to signing the Yakama Treaty.[12] Throughout his life, Kamiakin maintained that he never signed the treaty but "touched the pen" as an act of peace and friendship to satisfy the wishes of "Owhi and Teias and the chiefs." In his mind, Kamiakin did not agree to the written provisions of the treaty but touched the top of the quill pen as a measure of peace demanded by others.[13]

In his account of the war, Lieutenant Kip fails to link the Walla Walla Council with the Plateau Indian War, but there is a direct and important connection between the council and the war. Treaties, white arrogance, and aggression encouraged many Indians to side with Kamiakin and other leaders opposed to whites. Throughout the Walla Walla Council, the Indian leadership had commented that they should return to their people to discuss surrendering their land and living on reservations. Walla Walla Chief Peopeo Moxmox (Yellow Bird) requested "another meeting" so that he could have time to council with his people, but Stevens and Palmer knew that if the council broke up, the people would likely not agree to the treaties.[14] In June 1855, the Americans pushed the Indians into three treaties and onto reservations. As Stevens's former secretary George Gibbs stated, the "greatest single blunder" committed by Stevens was "cramming a treaty down their throats in a hurry."[15] American Indian policy required treaties and reservations, but Stevens created a hostile climate that culminated in war.

Stevens had assured the Indians that the government would not ratify the treaties for a few years. The governor was correct, since the Senate ratified the agreements in 1859. However, before leaving the council, Stevens penned newspaper dispatches opening eastern Washington and Oregon to white settlement.[16] When whites discovered gold near present-day Colville, Washington, miners migrated across Yakama country enroute to the diggings in violation of the agreement. Already angered that their leaders had signed the treaties, some Indians eagerly joined Kamiakin and Qualchin (spelled "Qualchien" by Kip, Owhi's son and Kamiakin's cousin) who had been recruiting Northwestern Indians to prepare for war.[17] At the end of his work, Kip records correctly that Kamiakin and Qualchin opposed the white invasion and rallied many Indians of the Pacific Northwest to fight.

War between the Indians of the Plateau and the United

States began in the summer of 1855. After the gold dis-
covery at Colville, miners moving through the Yakama
country raped and murdered Indians while stealing
horses.[18] In a letter sent to Maj. Gabriel Rains, Kamiakin
stated, "The Americans who were going to the mines shot
some Indians because they did not want to give them their
wives."[19] Qualchin found some of the culprits and executed
them, causing an investigation by Yakama Agent Andrew
Jackson Bolon. When Bolon arrived in the Yakama country, Kamiakin's brother, Showaway, warned him to leave
since his life was in danger.[20] Bolon took a less-traveled
trail back to The Dalles, but along the way, fell in with
some Yakamas. According to Suelel Lil, a fourteen-year-
old who witnessed the event, Mosheel and Wahpiqahpilah
killed Bolon, but many whites blamed Kamiakin and
Qualchin.[21]

Word of the agent's murder triggered the Plateau Indian War, a conflict sometimes referred to as the Yakama
War but one which involved far more than Yakama Indians. Between 1855 and 1857, the Indians fought what
they considered a defensive war against volunteer and
regular troops. After the Indians scored initial victories
in 1855, Major Rains attacked the people, driving many
from the Yakama country. Volunteers extended the war
into the lands of Walla Wallas, Cayuses, Umatillas,
Palouses, and Nez Perces.[22] White invasions brought many
diverse Indians into the camp of those opposing the United
States. When volunteers moved across the Walla Walla
Valley, Peopeo Moxmox rode in with a flag of truce and
surrendered to Col. James K. Kelly. While he was held
captive, Kelly allowed his volunteers to murder and dis-
member the venerated leader.[23]

To solidify their gains and announce their dominance
in the inland Northwest, the army built Forts Walla Walla
and Simcoe in the heart of Walla Walla and Yakama lands.
Not long after the establishment of Fort Walla Walla,
Palouses led by Tilcoax (Tilkohitz) stole the post's horse
herd. White accounts often blamed Kamiakin for the raid,

but Kip correctly identified Tilcoax as the raider, a fact verified by contemporary Indians. Tilcoax encouraged other Indians to harass the soldiers, which resulted in the killing of two miners near present-day Colfax, Washington.[24] By 1858, Kamiakin had moved to the Palouse River, establishing a village among his father's people where Indians considered him a Palouse chief. He severed his close relationship with the Yakama leadership, but he continued to oppose whites. At the same time, Tilcoax, not Kamiakin, was far more aggressive until Col. Edward J. Steptoe invaded the Indian country north of Snake River.[25]

In May 1858, Steptoe rode north to awe the tribes and quell native disturbances against gold miners near Fort Colville. Rather than take the native trail and newly surveyed military route running north from Fort Walla Walla to the Spokane River—surveyed by Lt. John Mullan, a man often mentioned by Kip—Steptoe rode east into Nez Perce country. Chief Tammutsa (known to whites as Timothy), his brother Levi, and thirteen other Nez Perces joined Steptoe's march into the rolling Palouse Hills between the Snake and Spokane rivers. Tammutsa was a Christian Indian and archenemy of Tilcoax. Indian runners had informed the soldiers not to enter this region, and Tammutsa knew this.[26] Steptoe entered this dangerous area ill prepared for battle, for although he brought one hundred and fifty-two men, five officers, and two mountain howitzers, each man carried only forty rounds of ammunition. Steptoe had ordered his men to leave their sabers behind, believing he would face minor opposition. Kip failed to mention that Steptoe was ill prepared, but the army never forgot that Steptoe had erred, costing American lives.[27] Kip purposely used his account to enhance Steptoe's reputation and put the best spin on the defeat.

The Steptoe disaster led Gen. Newman Clarke to order Col. George Wright to punish the warring tribes of the Columbia Plateau. Wright was not a newcomer to the region or the people. In 1856, he had negotiated with Owhi, Teias, Qualchin, Kamiakin, and others, but native leaders had never concluded an agreement with him.[28] Wright had confidently announced that he had ended the war, and he never forgave the leaders for not returning to conclude a peace (when they met again in 1858, Wright mentioned this fact to Owhi, see below). Kip briefly mentions this issue, but the account is far more helpful in reconstructing the movement of supplies and troops from Arizona, southern California, northern California, and Oregon to the Columbia River where the army deployed them from Fort Vancouver to either Fort Simcoe or Fort Walla Walla.

Clarke and Wright assembled a large army that was well provisioned so that it could defeat the Yakamas, Palouses, Cayuses, Sincayuses, Spokanes, Wanapums, Walla Wallas, Okanogans, Coeur d'Alenes, and others. Kip's account notes that troops under Maj. Robert Garnett and three hundred additional men moved north into the Yakama country before heading east. The plan was for Garnett to push the Indians east onto the Plateau south of the Spokane River. Kip provides little about Garnett, but in an oral history, Mary Moses (Owhi's daughter, Qualchin's sister, and wife of Chief Quetalakin or Moses) stated that a small group of leaders and their families fled the Wenatchi country because of Garnett. She stated that Garnett drove many "Indians into hiding" and stole "horses, cattle, and equipment away from them."[29]

Kip's account does not deal with Garnett's expedition, since Kip traveled to Fort Walla Walla and remained with the main branch of the army under Colonel Wright. Kip left Walla Walla on August 7, 1858, serving under Capt. E. D. Keyes whom Wright had ordered to build a supply depot named Fort Taylor on the Snake River. He provides an account of this preliminary movement of troops to Snake River and their encounters with their "bold and insulting" enemy who warned the soldiers not to cross the river. Kip's account of Wright's march north across the Plateau, the Battle of Four Lakes, and the Battle of Spokane Plain is the best written documentation of these events. Although Wright's reports on the war are available (provided here in the appendix), they are not as detailed or as colorful as that provided by Kip.[30]

The young lieutenant was in the heat of battle, fighting in the vanguard, and carefully recording the movement of soldiers and warriors. When the Indians engaged the army in the Battle of Four Lakes, located near present-day Cheney, Washington, a site just west of Spokane, Kip fought throughout the campaign and shortly thereafter composed his account of the fight. "Every spot seemed alive with the wild warriors," Kip wrote, and the Indians rode "fleet, hardy horses . . . brandishing their weapons, shouting their war cries, and keeping up a song of defiance." Kip's account of the fight is wonderfully written in flowing prose that invites readers to engage the narrative.[31]

Four days after the first fight, the Indians fought the army in the Battle of Spokane Plain. On September 5, 1858, Native Americans began dogging the troops, riding parallel to them and setting fire to the bunch grass. "Under cover of the smoke," Kip recorded, "they formed round us in one-third of a circle, and poured in their fire." Thus began the battle in which Indians raced "down a hill five hundred feet high and with a slope of forty-five degrees." Although the Indians fought gallantly, the army "swept the enemy before them" using long range Harper's Ferry, Springfield, and Sharp's rifles.[32] The various bands regrouped and fought again, but in the end, they fled in disarray, each group determining its own course of action.

"We learned afterwards," Kip wrote, "that Kamiakien, the great war chief of the Yakimas, was almost killed. A shell bust in the tree above him, tearing off a branch which struck him on the head." This intelligence was correct, for family member Emily Peone recounted in 1981 that Kamiakin fell from his horse after a limb struck him in

the head. His youngest wife Colestah was by his side,
and she rescued the leader, riding away to a safe spot
where she doctored him.[33]

The aftermath of the Battle of Spokane Plain is graphi-
cally and accurately presented by Kip who details the
slaughter of nine hundred Indian horses, animals that
did not belong to Tilcoax as suggested by Kip but to two
Palouses from Wawawai, Poyahkin and Penockahlowyun
(Whistling Bird).[34] Kip also describes the councils Wright
held with prominent native leaders along the present-
day boundary of Washington and Idaho. He details
Wright's request that leaders come into council, telling
Indian runners that no one would be harmed. According
to Mary Moses, Spokan Garry and Big Star told the leaders to go to Wright and "make a treaty of peace and Col.
Wright certainly led the Indians to believe that those who
came to the conference would be received as under a flag
of truce."[35] Kip failed to mention the treachery of Wright
in inviting leaders to surrender peacefully and then hanging some of them or the foul play of inviting families to a
peace council where whites took women and children captive.

Kip provides the most detailed account of Wright's
treachery in capturing Owhi and Qualchin's hanging.
Owhi rode to Wright's camp with the intention of negotiating in good faith, and not long afterwards, Qualchin
did the same, not knowing that Wright held Owhi captive. According to Kip, Wright admonished Owhi for not
completing their negotiations in 1856 and soon ordered
his soldiers to take him prisoner. Kip records that within
fifteen minutes Owhi's son, Qualchin, came in to talk
peace with his wife and another man (Lo Kout), and
Wright ordered his men to seize Qualchin and hang him
immediately. In the confusion, Qualchin realized that
Wright had captured his father.

Kip wrote that while Qualchin struggled, he denounced
Kamiakin and "died like a coward." Kip maintained that
Owhi disowned his son, saying that Qualchin was

Kamiakin's son. Members of the Owhi and Kamiakin families refute Kip's statements and point out that Kip could not speak Yakama. Qualchin's sister, Mary Moses, was camped nearby when the soldiers hanged Qualchin, and years later she "stated that she could not believe" that "the last words of Qualchien were curses on Kamiakin" because the two men had always been good friends who had helped each other. Perhaps Qualchin called out for Kamiakin's help since he was known to be in the area, but there is no native tradition that Qualchin condemned Kamiakin or that Owhi disowned his son.[36]

Kip provides Wright's words at the various councils, including the colonel's statement, "if I come here again to war, I will hang them all, men, women, and children." Wright threatened the people with extermination, and contemporary Native Americans claim that they believed him given his slaughter of horses. Indians reasoned that any human who could slay so many stallions, mares, fillies, and colts could just as easily exterminate recalcitrant Indians. Kip notes that Wright had Owhi shot to death while trying to escape and hanged at least fifteen warriors, including several Palouses who had followed Kamiakin and Slowiarchy.[37]

Throughout the book, Kamiakin emerges as a prominent leader from the proceedings at the Walla Walla Council to the army's return to Fort Walla Walla. Kip describes Kamiakin as "the most powerful chief" and a "relentless enemy of the whites." This is an accurate characterization of Kamiakin, who Kip remarked held "the same position with them that Tecumpsah formerly did with our north-western tribes." In much the same way as Tecumseh, Kamiakin formed a short-lived Indian confederacy. Sahaptin-, Salishan-, and Chinookan-speaking Indians united to stand in a military and political alliance to defeat whites. And just as Tenskwatawa had led the religious revitalization movement among Indians of the Old Northwest, Wanapum holy man Smohalla did the same in the New Northwest during the 1850s and 1860s, while many other spiritual leaders also denounced the Americans, Christianity, materialism, and the reservation system.[38]

Kip states that during Wright's councils with the tribes, Spokan Garry and Big Star tried to convince Kamiakin to surrender. Kamiakin refused to give up because "he was afraid he should be taken to Walla Walla." Emily Peone stated that twice Kamiakin rode toward Wright's camp to discuss peace, but both times he believed Wright would hang him, so he never surrendered. Given Wright's actions against the native leadership, Kamiakin was probably correct. Kamiakin rode into Canada and moved south into Montana to live with Flatheads. Later, he considered surrendering at Fort Walla Walla but had a premonition that the army would hang him. According to Peone, Kamiakin had psychic abilities and saw things before they happened. In the early 1860s, Kamiakin's band returned to live at their village on the Palouse River and, later, at Rock Lake where the chief died in 1877.[39]

Kamiakin's power waned after the Plateau Indian War of 1858, as did tribal power throughout the region. As Kip put it, "Indian tribes, hitherto so troublesome and defiant, have been entirely subjected." The United States forced many non-reservation Indians onto the reservations and opened their former homes to white settlers. Indeed, Kip notes that an "immense tract of splendid country . . . is now opened to the white man . . . without danger from their former savage foe." However, native resistance to white rule never ended. The broader history of Northwestern Indians is shared with native people throughout the United States, but the particulars of the conquest and its consequences to individuals and groups differ dramatically from place to place. Kip provides a useful historical account of the last phases of the war and Wright's handling of Indian affairs following the conflict.

Kip's *Indian War in the Pacific Northwest* is a moving account that reflects the Manifest Destiny of the United States, and the belief of Kip's contemporaries that they had a God-given right to negotiate treaties with the tribes, destroy the people militarily, hang native patriots for fighting in the war, take women and children hostage, threaten the people with extermination, and establish American rule in Indian country. This book is a revealing and useful document, filled with colorful narratives and generally accurate representations that shed a great deal of light on American Indian policy during the late 1850s in the Pacific Northwest. The book, first published in 1859, will be of great use to anyone interested in the frontier army, Native American resistance to white rule, and the broader spectrum of Northwestern history.

NOTES

1. Andrew George, oral interview by Clifford E. Trafzer, Richard D. Scheuerman, and Lee Ann Smith, Yakama Reservation, 15 November 1980.

2. Lawrence Kip, *Army Life on the Pacific* (1859; reprint Fairfield WA: Ye Galleon Press, 1986), i–iii.

3. Frederick Merk, *Manifest Destiny and Mission in American History* (New York: Vintage Books, 1963), 24–34, 261–66. Merk differentiates the two concepts by characterizing Manifest Destiny as an aggressive, often violent movement that uses force to accomplish Americanization, while he interprets Mission to be a more benign form of American activity, including civilization and Christianization programs supported by the United States.

4. Alvin Josephy Jr., *The Nez Perce and the Opening of the Pacific Northwest* (New Haven: Yale University Press, 1965), 43–68, 220, 226–40; Robert Ruby and John Brown, *The Cayuse Indians* (Norman: University of Oklahoma Press, 1972), 23–25, 84–112; Robert I. Burns, *The Jesuits and the Indian Wars of the Northwest* (New Haven: Yale University Press, 1966), 13, 647–58.

5. Kent D. Richards, *Isaac I. Stevens: Young Man in a Hurry* (Provo UT: Brigham Young University Press, 1979), 98–99; A. J. Splawn, *Ka-mi-akin: Last Hero of the Yakimas* (Portland OR: Stationary and Printing Company, 1917), 19; William C. Brown,

The Indian Side of the Story (Spokane: C. W. Hill Printers, 1961), 60–80.

6. Kamiakin to the soldiers, 7 October 1855, Click Relander Collection, Yakima Valley Regional Library, Yakima WA; original found in the Archives of the Diocese of Seattle, Seattle WA. Kamiakin dictated this letter to Father Charles M. Pandosy who spoke Yakama, French, and English. He interpreted Kamiakin's words, composed the letter, and sent it to Major Rains. This is the reason the letter is in the Diocean Archives.

7. Kip uses the term, Chipunish, to describe the Nez Perces. Meriwether Lewis and William Clark referred to the people as Choppunish, which may be the origin of the term used commonly by whites in the early nineteenth century.

8. Nez Perce people have always called themselves *Nimipu*, the people. The word first appeared in the creation story of the people when Coyote killed the monster and used his body parts to make Native Americans and the blood from the heart to make *Nimipu*.

9. David L. Nicandri, *Northwest Chiefs: Gustavus Sohon's Views of the 1855 Stevens Treaty Council* (Tacoma: Washington State Historical Society, 1986); report of Gustavus Sohon in John Mullan, "Report of Lieutenant Mullan, in charge of the Construction of the Military Road from Fort Walla Walla to Fort Benton," *House Executive Document* (hereafter *HED*) 44, 36th Cong., 2d Sess., Serial Set (hereafter SS) 1099.

10. Clifford E. Trafzer and Richard D. Scheuerman, *Renegade Tribe: The Palouse Indians and the Invasion of the Inland Pacific Northwest* (Pullman: Washington State University Press, 1986), 42–45, 57–59.

11. Andrew D. Pambrun, *Sixty Years on the Frontier in the Pacific Northwest* (edited by Edward J. Kowrach, Fairfield WA: Ye Galleon Press, 1978), 94–96.

12. "Documents Relating to Negotiations of Ratified and Unratified Treaties of the United States," National Archives (hereafter NA), Record Group 75, Microfilm T494, Reel 5, hereafter cited as Council Proceedings, 1855; "Doty's Journal of Operations" in Council Proceedings, 1855; Splawn, *Ka-mi-akin*, 32–33; Brown, *The Indian Side of the Story*, 85–130; Richards, *Isaac I. Stevens*, 215–26.

13. Council Proceedings, 1855; Trafzer and Scheuerman, *Renegade Tribe*, 58–59, 158.

14. Council Proceedings, 1855.

15. Gibbs to Swan, 8 January 1857, *The Northwest Coast: or, Three Year's Residence in Washington Territory*, James G. Swan (New York: Harper and Brothers, 1857), 428.

16. Trafzer and Scheuerman, *Renegade Tribe*, 61; for an example of a newspaper account, see *Oregon Weekly Times*, 23 June 1855.

17. Trafzer and Scheuerman, *Renegade Tribe*, 62–64, 66.

18. Kamiakin to the soldiers, 7 October 1855; Mason to Rains, 26 September 1855, Archives of the Washington State Library, Olympia WA; Granville O. Haller, "The Indian War of 1855–1856," Manuscript Collection, University of Washington Library; Granville O. Haller, "Kamiakin—In History: Memoir of the War, in the Yakima Valley, 1855–1856," Manuscript A 128, Bancroft Library, University of California, Berkeley. The miners killed included Cummings, Fanjoy, Huffman, Jamison, and Walker.

19. Kamiakin to the soldiers, 7 October 1855.

20. Mason to Maloney, 24 September 1855, NA, Records of the United States Army Commands (hereafter RUSAC), Record Group 393, Letters Received (hereafter LR); L. V. McWhorter, *Tragedy of the Wahk-shum: Prelude to the Yakima Indian War, 1855–1856: the Killing of Major Andrew Jackson Bolon* (Fairfield WA: Ye Galleon Press, 1958), 4–5; D'Herbonez to Brouillet, 28 August 1854, Archives of the Diocese of Seattle, Seattle WA.

21. McWhorter, *Tragedy of the Wahk-shum*, 4–5.

22. Wool to Thomas, 19 October 1855, *HED* 93, 34th Cong., 1st Sess., SS 858; Cain to Mannypenny, 6 October 1855, NA, Washington Superintendency, Record Group 75, LR.

23. William N. Bischoff, "The Yakima Indian War, 1855–1856" (Ph.D. diss., Loyola University of Chicago, 1950); Kelly to Adjutant General, 1 March 1856, Wilson to Farrar, 15 June 1856, Pillow to Farrar, 18 June and 20 August 1856, Raymond to Farrar, 14 November 1856, Kelly to Curry, 15 January 1856, Bates to Farrar, 19 June 1856, Curry to Davis, 19 January and 12 April 1856, Layton to Farrar, 18 June 1856, NA, RUSAC, Record Group 393, LR (a copy of Layton to Farrar is also in the Layton Papers, Oregon Historical Society, Portland); Kelly to Farrar, 14 December 1855, *Portland Oregonian*, 5 January 1856; Wool to Thomas, 25 December 1855 and Wool to Stevens, 2

February 1856, *HED* 93, 34th Cong., 1st Sess., SS 858; Wool to Wright, 20 January 1856, NA, RUSAC, Record Group 393, Letters Sent; T. C. Elliott, "The Murder of Peu-Peu-Mox-Mox," *Oregon Historical Quarterly* 16 (1915): 123–30; Clarence L. Andrews, "Warfield's Story of Peo-Peo-Mox-Mox," *Washington Historical Quarterly* 25 (1934): 182–84; J. F. Santee, "The Slaying of Pio-Pio-Mox-Mox," *Washington Historical Quarterly* 25 (1934): 128–32. For a detailed discussion of volunteer attacks against the Palouses, Cayuses, Umatillas, Walla Wallas, and Nez Perces, see Trafzer and Scheuerman, *Renegade Tribe,* 68–71, 73–75.

24. Steptoe to Mackall, 17 April 1858, *Senate Executive Document* (hereafter *SED*) 1, 35th Cong., 2nd Sess., SS 975; Trafzer and Scheuerman, *Renegade Tribe,* 76.

25. Other Palouse leaders, including Mahkeetahkat and Slowiarchy the Younger, attacked the miners near Colfax, but Tilcoax encouraged many diverse Indians to retaliate against whites who crossed north of Snake River. See Owen to Nesmith, 16 July 1858, *Annual Report of the Commissioner of Indian Affairs, 1858* (Washington DC: Office of Indian Affairs, Department of the Interior, 1958), 269–71; Trafzer and Scheuerman, *Renegade Tribe,* 76–78.

26. Robert I. Burns, "Pere Joset's Account of the Indian War of 1858," *Pacific Northwest Quarterly* 38 (1947): 293–95, 301; Trafzer and Scheuerman, *Renegade Tribe,* 49–50, 77–78, 82–84.

27. Seven soldiers died in the Steptoe Battle, including two officers, Lt. William Gaston and Capt. Oliver Hazard Taylor for whom the soldiers named Fort Taylor. The Indians severely wounded six soldiers and slightly wounded seven others. In addition, the Indians killed three Nez Perce scouts who served with the army.

28. Trafzer and Scheuerman, *Renegade Tribe,* 71–73.

29. Mary Moses, oral interview by Judge William C. Brown, Brown Collection, Manuscript, Archives, and Special Collections, Holland Library, Washington State University (hereafter WSU), Pullman.

30. Wright to Mackall, 31 August, 1 September, and 2 September 1858, and John Mullan, "Topographical Memoir and Map of Colonel Wright's Campaign Against the Indians of Oregon and Washington Territories," *SED* 32, 35th Cong., 2nd Sess., SS 984.

31. Trafzer and Scheuerman, *Renegade Tribe*, 86–88.

32. Trafzer and Scheuerman, *Renegade Tribe*, 84; Burns, *The Jesuits and the Indian Wars of the Northwest*, 241.

33. Emily Peone, oral interviews by Richard D. Scheuerman, Colville Indian Reservation, January–June, 1981. Note that many spellings exist for Native American names and tribes. The spelling from the original document is retained in the quotations, but in the text the modern spelling of names and preferred spelling of tribes as stated by certain native nations are used.

34. Brown, *The Indian Side of the Story*, 252–56.

35. Mary Moses, interview.

36. Mary Moses, interview.

37. Mary Moses, interview; Trafzer and Scheuerman, *Renegade Tribe*, 90–92.

38. Clifford E. Trafzer and Margery Ann Beach, "Smohalla, the Washani, and Religion as a Factor in Northwestern Indian History," *American Indian Quarterly* 9 (1985): 309–16.

39. Winans to Partee, 18 November 1870, Winans's Reports, N 34, Box 147–4, Winans Collection, WSU; Sophie Williams, oral interview by Click Relander, "Colville and Palouse Notes," 45, Relander Collection, Yakima Valley Regional Library, Yakima WA; Splawn, *Ka-mi-akin*, 8, 9, 121, 123, 409; Trafzer and Scheuerman, *Renegade Tribe*, 93–97, 100–102.

CONTENTS.

APPENDIX.

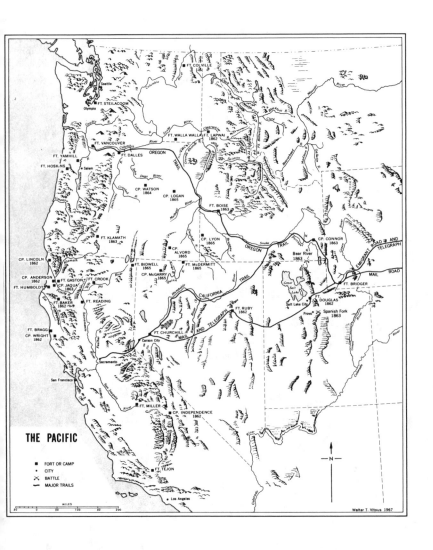

THE PACIFIC

- ■ FORT OR CAMP
- • CITY
- ✕ BATTLE
- — MAJOR TRAILS

MILES

Walter T. Vitous 1967

PREFACE.

The following pages are merely a journal kept during the expedition it attempts to describe, and afterwards prepared for the press. It is an attempt to show the manner in which such an expedition is conducted, and to picture some phases of " Army Life."

It is the tendency in this country to decry the services of the army and of its officers ; and yet, most of the latter spend the greater part of their lives on the frontiers and in the Indian country. Weeks at a time are passed in scouting against their treacherous foe, enduring every hardship, and daily risking life itself, to open the way for the pioneer and settler. Yet, what is their reward ? When the papers come to them from the regions of civilization, they find themselves stigmatized in editorials, and even in speeches on the floor of Congress, as the drones of society, living on the government, yet a useless encumbrance and expense.

But, one by one, how many lay down their lives in this cause ! Without counting those who sink into the grave from sickness produced by unwholesome climates, exposure and hardships, how many more actually meet their deaths on the battle field ! During the last season alone, Taylor, Gaston, Allen and Van Camp have thus shed their blood, and every year the list increases. Yet they fall in battle with an obscure enemy, and little are their sufferings appreciated by the

> —————" gentlemen
> Who live at home at ease."

Of the exposure and hardships, indeed, of our Army, the present jour nal furnishes no fit illustration, for the country in which the expedition was undertaken is comparatively a healthy one. The story is far different when the scene is among the Everglades of Florida, the burning heats on the Colorado, or the mountain passes of the Apaches. Yet these pages may give some idea of the nature of these expeditions, and the manner in which they are conducted.

Of the two battles the descriptions are necessarily very general, while for the benefit of the professional reader, the Official Reports have been printed in the Appendix.

These pages having been printed while the writer is on the other side of the continent, he would avail himself of this means of returning his thanks to George L. Duyckinck, Esq., for his kindness and the trouble he has taken in carrying them through the Press.

Fort Vancouver, W. T., December 7th, 1858.

I.

ORIGIN OF THE WAR.

CHAPTER I.

ORIGIN, OF THE WAR.

HE month of May, 1858, was a disastrous one for the army on the Pacific. On the 8th, Colonel Steptoe set out from Fort Walla Walla, with a small command of one hundred and fifty-nine men, to make a reconnaisance of the country, to examine into affairs at Fort Colville, and to seize some marauders belonging to the Pelouze tribe, who had stolen cattle from the Fort. As this is a feeble tribe, his force was considered quite sufficient to overawe them, while the more powerful tribes through which he was to pass had always professed friendship, and there had been as yet no reason to distrust them.

On the morning of the 16th, however, after passing Snake river, he found himself unexpectedly in the face of a force estimated at from one thousand to fifteen hundred Indians. They were Spokans, Pelouzes, Cœur d'Alenes, Yakimas, and warriors of the smaller tribes, all painted and in their war dress, evidently meditating an attack. The hills around were covered with them, and it being evidently impossible under such circumstances to penetrate into the country, it became necessary for his little command to return, and endeavor to make good its way back to Snake river. The train was therefore closed up,

2

and a retrograde move begun. The moment this was done, the attack commenced, and the fight was kept up through the whole day. Most of the men, too, were new recruits, who had never before been under fire. Yet everything that could be done by the officers was accomplished. It was a series of gallant charges, driving the Indians back with loss, to have them after a brief interval close up again around the troops.

Night at last settled down upon the battle field, and found the little command perfectly exhausted, and with their ammunition almost gone. Two officers,—Captain Oliver H. P. Taylor and Lieutenant William Gaston, both of the First Dragoons,—had fallen, with a number of the men. The remainder were gathered on a rising ground, while every hill around swarmed with their exulting enemies, who seemed to have them now completely in their toils. A consultation of the officers was hastily held by Colonel Steptoe, at which there was but one opinion. The force against them was overpowering, and by the next morning would undoubtedly be still further increased: without ammunition they would be almost defenceless,—and it was evident, that long before the close of the next day, not one of the command would be left to tell the story of their fight.

Nothing remained, therefore, but to attempt a retreat during the night. The bodies of the fallen, which were within their reach, were buried,—the two howitzers were *cached*,*—and the command mounted and struck off in the direction of Snake river. Fortunately the Indians did not make a night attack, and their retreat was unimpeded.

---

* This is a word introduced by the first Canadian (French) *voyageurs* and trappers. Pits were dug, where they deposited provisions, or other things, and they were carefully covered so as to conceal all traces from the Indians. They thus often remained for months till reopened by their owners.

Still, they knew that the morning would bring their foes upon their track, and therefore they pressed on. They rode seventy-five miles by ten o'clock the next morning, and succeeded in crossing the river without the further loss of a single man, or even of an animal belonging to the command. Here Colonel Steptoe was met by Captain Dent, who, having received intelligence of the ambush, was advancing by forced marches from Fort Walla Walla to his rescue.

Among those who were reported as "missing" after the fight, were two non-commissioned officers. They were both wounded, but escaped from the Indians; and finding that the command had retreated, commenced their own return on foot. Fortunately the Indians next day did not follow them, being probably engaged in the division of plunder, and their attention directed to the main body of the retreating command. After several days they reached the river, where they were seized by the Indians on its banks. One of them,—Sergeant Williams,—they killed, but permitted the other to cross the river, and he finally reached Walla Walla in safety.

Such is a brief history of this unfortunate affair. I have recurred to it, because it is appropriately the opening chapter of the campaign, and indeed the cause and origin of all our operations through the ensuing season. In the newspapers, too,—many of which are always ready to decry the regular army,—the greatest injustice has been done to this gallant little party. Surprised by an over-powering hostile force, they fought it out gallantly as long as fighting was practicable, and then made their retreat without any additional loss.

The Indians of these northern tribes are the most bold and warlike on the continent. Splendid specimens of physical humanity, they are skilful in the use of arms,

and accustomed from childhood almost to live on horseback.   They have seen but little of the whites, except
a few straggling miners who during the last year may
have passed through their country, and the *employés* of
the Hudson Bay Company, from whom they purchase
their muskets and ammunition.   For years it has been the
object of the latter to inculcate upon them reverence for
themselves, and a proportionate contempt for the Americans.   The fight with Colonel Steptoe of course confirmed
this impression, and brought out all the smouldering feeling of hostility which had before been excited by their
fears of the future encroachments of the whites.   In fact,
the attack on Colonel Steptoe was probably produced by
the news they had received of Lieutenant Mullan's party
being on their way to survey and lay out a military road
through their country.   This they regarded as the first
step in taking possession of their lands.

The result was natural.   At once a league was formed
of all the most powerful tribes,—the Spokans, Cœur
d'Alenes, Pelouzes and Yakimas, with a portion of the
Nez Percés;—a general outbreak took place, small parties of whites were cut off in every part of the country, and
even the safety of Fort Walla Walla was threatened.   The
Indians became everywhere bold, defiant, and insulting.

With the limited force on this coast, scattered in small
parties over fifteen hundred miles, it was of course difficult
to meet the exigency.   Troops had to be withdrawn from
posts at the South where they really were needed.   Yet
every possible step was promptly taken by General Clarke.
As soon as expresses could reach them, companies were
converging to the hostile country from every part of the
Pacific coast, even from Fort Yuma on the far distant
banks of the Colorado, and from San Diego on the borders
of Mexico.

II.

DEPARTURE.

CHAPTER II.

AT this time I was in San Francisco, preparing to join my company at San Bernadino in Southern California, when I received orders from General Clarke to remain in the city, as my company would shortly be up, on its way to Oregon. Sunday morning, June 12th, it arrived in the steamer *Senator*, and being transferred to the *Pacific*, I at once reported for duty and went on board.

Monday was a busy day. The soldiers, after their sea voyage, were naturally restless to visit the city, yet for fear of desertion they had to be watched and confined to the steamer. Military stores of all kinds were to be taken on board,—provisions, ammunition, cannon, and a lot of mules. The embarkation of the latter was by no means easy. It required the most forcible arguments to induce them to march up the plank, and one so successfully evaded it, as to drop himself into the water, to the infinite delight of the countless idlers around. Swimming out beyond the wharf into the bay, he seemed to have no settled plan for the future, and so commenced going round in a circle, an amusement which he continued until he was lassoed and dragged again on the wharf. The officers found themselves fully occupied in attempting to keep order in this scene of confusion.

At three in the afternoon we managed to get under way. The command on board consisted of companies A, G, and M, of the Third Artillery, and the following officers:

Captain, Erasmus D. Keyes.

First Lieutenant, Robert O. Tyler.
    "   "   James L. White.
    "   "   Dunbar R. Ransom.

Second Lieutenant, Hylan B. Lyon.
    "   "   Geo. F. B. Dandy.
    "   "   Lawrence Kip.

Our voyage was a long one, as the coal was bad and we ran slowly. It was not until Friday, the 18th, that we crossed the bar at the mouth of the Columbia river,—from its shifting shoals the most dangerous navigation on the whole Pacific coast. A short distance up the river stands Astoria, rendered classical ground by Washington Irving. An old trapper still living, who belonged to Mr. Astor's first party, says he has often seen one thousand Indian canoes at a time collected on the beach in front of the fort. When the Hudson Bay Company took charge of it, they removed their establishment up the river to Vancouver, and allowed the fort to fall into decay, till not a vestige of it now remains. A few houses, like the beginning of a village, are scattered along the banks which slope down to the river, wooded to the edge with pines.

At evening we reached Fort Vancouver. Near the river are low meadow grounds, on which stands the post of the Hudson Bay Company,—a picketed enclosure of about three hundred yards square, composed of roughly split pine logs. Within this are the buildings of the establishment, where much of its immense fur trade was once carried on. From these head quarters, their companies of trappers, hunters, and voyageurs, generally Canadians, were sent out to thread the rivers in pursuit of the beaver.   Alone they traversed the plains, or passed months in the defiles of the mountains, far north to the Russian possessions, or south to the borders of California, returning in one or two years with the furs, to barter at the fort.   Then came generally a short time of the wildest revelry, until everything was dissipated or perhaps gam. bled away, when with a new outfit they set forth on another expedition.   From Vancouver the company sent their cargoes of furs and peltries to England, and thence they received by sea their yearly supplies. They possessed an influence over the Indians which was wonderful, and which the perfect system of their operations enabled them for years to maintain.   But the transfer of the country to the Americans, and the progress of civilization around them driving off the Indians and beaver, have forced them to remove much of their business to other posts.

Fort Vancouver is probably the most pleasant of our posts on the Pacific coast.   The place is healthy and the scenery around beautiful, furnishing opportunities of fishing, hunting, and riding, while its nearness to Portland and Oregon City prevents the young officers from being, as at many other western posts, deprived of the refining influence of female society.   Many are the occasions on which they find it necessary to drop down to these places.   Deserters are supposed to be lurking there, garrison stores are to be provided, or some other of Uncle Sam's interests are to be looked after.   Then, these visits must be returned, for the inhabitants of these places have an equal care for the welfare of their neighbors at the fort.   Numerous, therefore, are the parties of pleasure which come from these towns to enliven the solitude of the garrison. On these occasions they are welcomed by balls, and night after night music is heard floating over the waters of the Columbia river, and the brilliant glare of lights from the fort shows that *tattoo* is not the signal for all within its walls to retire.

2*

On landing, the officers were distributed around, while Lieutenant White and myself were indebted for our quarters to the hospitality of Major Alvord.

When I was here, three years ago, the post was quiet enough, there being but three companies stationed at it. Now it is as lively as can be, being the landing-place of all those on their way to the seat of war, and where they are equipped for the field ;—constant drills going on, and nothing but hurry and preparation from morning to night. The rattle of the drum and the notes of the bugle are the constant sounds we hear.

June 20*th*.—Had a general review to-day. Lieutenant Colonel Morris, (Fourth Infantry), who commands the post, inspected our companies, together with those stationed here.

June 21*st*.—Captain Keyes, with companies A and M, left this morning for the Dalles. My company must wait until next week for the arrival of the *Columbia*, as she brings up arms and ammunition, and the men must be equipped anew, before they can go into the field. Colonel George Wright, (Ninth Infantry), will take command of the expedition, while Captain Keyes will have command of the Artillery Companies in the field. Six companies of the Third Artillery will be collected at Fort Walla Walla ; a larger number of the regiment than have been together since they were wrecked, five years ago, on the ill-fated steamer *San Francisco*.

June 23*rd*.—Last night the steamer arrived, bringing General Clarke and Staff, Captain Kirkham, Quarter-master, Lieutenant Walker, A. D. C., and Lieutenant Sill, of the Ordnance Corps. They stopped at Umqua, and took in Company B, of the Third Artillery, commanded by Lieutenants George P. Ihrie and James Howard. A salute of eleven guns was fired this morning for General Clarke. Colonels Wright and Steptoe are ordered down to Fort Vancouver to have a consultation with General Clarke.

This morning our company left Fort Vancouver in the steamer for the Dalles; the officers, Lieutenants White, Ransom, and myself. It is about fifty miles to the Cascades. The scenery of the river is in all parts beautiful, but very varied in its character. The pine forests stretch down to the banks, enlivened here and there by the cultivated spot which some settler has cleared, whose axe awakened new and strange echoes as it rang through the primeval woods. On the margin of the shore, and particularly on one of the islands, we noticed the dead-houses of the Indians, rudely constructed of logs. Within, the bodies of the deceased are placed for a time, attired in their best array, until the building becomes filled. Then the oldest occupants are removed and placed on the shore, till the tide launches them off on their last voyage, and they are swept down to the ocean, which to the "untutored savage" as to his more cultivated brethren, symbolizes Eternity.

When a chief dies, his body is sometimes wrapped in a blanket and suspended between two trees, as if swinging in a hammock. We saw one which had already remained in that situation more than six months.

At six in the evening we reached the Cascades, the head of navigation. Here a *portage* has to be made, as the river for more than two miles flows over the rocks, whirling and boiling in a succession of rapids similar to those in the river St. Lawrence. This is the great salmon fishery of the Columbia river, the season for which is in the spring, when the fish ascend the river in incredible numbers. The banks are inhabited by the remains of the Indian tribes, (most of them having been removed to the Indian Reservations,) who display their skill in catching the salmon, which they dry for exportation. Little bridges are thrown out over the rocks, on which the Indians post themselves, with nets on hoops, to which long handles are attached.

With these they scoop up the fish and throw them on the shore. They are then pounded fine between two stones, cured, and tightly packed in bales of grass matting lined with dried fish-skin, in which state they will keep for years. The process is now precisely the same as it was when described by Lewis and Clarke. The aboriginal village of Wishram, at the head of the narrows, which they mention as being the place of resort for the tribes from the interior to barter for fish, is yet in existence. We still notice, too, the difference which those early explorers observed, between these Indians and those of the plains. The latter, living on horseback, are finely developed, and look like warriors ; the former, engaged only in their canoes, or stooping over the banks, are low in stature, and seem to have been dwarfed out of all manhood. In every thing noble they are many degrees below the wild tribes on the plains.

At the Cascades the men were landed, and camped for the night, while the officers were supplied with quarters by Lieutenant Mallory, (Fourth Infantry), who has command of the company stationed at this post. During the last Indian war, three years ago, this little settlement was surprised and almost entirely destroyed by the Indians.

June 24*th*.—In the morning we marched the men about four miles, across the portage, and embarked in another little steamer which was to carry us to the Dalles. The scenery above was similar to that which we had already passed. In one place the mountains seem to come down to the river, ending in a huge rock perfectly steep, which has received the name of Cape Horn. Above, the precipices are covered with fir and white cedar; two small cascades, like silver lines, leap from point to point for a distance of one hundred and fifty feet, while below, in the deep shadow, the waters sweep around the rocks with a sullen sound. About six in the evening we reached the Dalles.

III.

FORT DALLES AND THE MARCH.

CHAPTER III.

FORT DALLES AND THE MARCH.

HEN last I saw this post, three years since, it seemed to me to be the most unattractive on the Pacific. Without even the beauty of scenery which surrounds Fort Vancouver, its sole recommendation was its healthiness. Nor did the Government buildings add anything to its appearance. Planned and erected some years ago by the Mounted Rifles, when they were stationed in Oregon, they were remarkably primitive, and very little attention had been bestowed upon their architecture. In those days, the ornamental had not yet been developed on the Pacific coast.

The change now is a great one, for during the past year new quarters have been erected, under the direction of Captain Jordan, Quarter-master, which are arranged in every way to promote the convenience of those for whom they are intended. The officers' quarters are in the cottage form, and for taste are superior to those we have seen at any other post.

On our arrival, my company, together with the three of the Third Artillery already there, camped about a quarter of a mile from the barracks, while the officers' tents were pitched a short distance from those of the men.

We at once commenced our regular routine. At nine

in the morning, we have dress parade; at half-past nine, we drill for an hour, (light infantry, Hardie's tactics); at twelve, the men are practiced at firing at a mark, and estimating distances; at five in the evening, we have drill; and at half-past six, guard mounting. Drilling, too, is a very different matter from what it is at a post in time of peace. Then, it is a sort of *pro forma* business, in which neither officers nor men take much interest. Now, it is invested with a reality, since all are conscious that our success in the field depends perhaps upon the state of discipline.

Still, there is time for sociability, and the *esprit du corps* which prevails in the Army, renders a meeting of officers of different regiments a delightful reunion. We have our mess in camp, but are constantly dining with the officers at the post. This is the head-quarters of the Ninth Infantry, and their band is an exceedingly fine one.

June 28th.—Colonel Steptoe arrived from Walla Walla, on his way to Vancouver; and on the same day, Major Mackall, Assistant Adjutant General, Major Allen, Quartermaster, and Captains Ingalls, Kirkham and Jordan, came up from Vancouver. They all returned in a couple of days, except Colonel Steptoe, and Captain Jordan who is stationed here.

June 30th.—Major Mackall reviewed us; after which we had muster. The officers are now mounted, and we are only waiting the arrival of the steamer with additional stores, to begin our march.

The news brought in from the country of the hostile Indians is, that they have made a league among themselves to carry on this war for five years. This they consider to be the last struggle in which they will have to engage, as in that time they can exterminate the whites.

July 7th.—At three in the afternoon we took leave of

the officers to whose hospitality we have been so much indebted, and commenced our march across the plains. The length of each day's march will have to be regulated by the water, which in some places is not to be found for a distance of twenty miles. The country over which we passed during the afternoon is barren and desolate, unfit for culture, except a few spots on the river. After a march of six miles, we reached Five Mile Creek, where we camped for the night.

Our time of starting in the morning depends on the length of the march before us. When it is to be a long one, we have *reveillé* at three o'clock in the morning, and get under way by five. With short marches, *reveillé* was at five, and we marched at seven. It takes two hours to pack up and get the command started. Through the twelve and a half days which it took to reach Walla Walla, our march varied from five to thirty miles a day.* The soldiers in marching average a mile in twenty minutes.

Our order of march was, to have two companies in advance,—then, the train,—then, two companies more,—then, a rear guard of twenty men behind, under a lieutenant, with the hospital wagon. Their duty was to pick

* We give the list of each day's march to Walla Walla:

July 7th. To Five Mile Creek,	6 miles.
" 8 " " Des Chutes,	10 "
" 9 " " Mud Springs,	11 "
" 10 " " Camp beyond John Day's River,	20 "
" 11 " " Rock Creek,	6 "
" 12 " " Willow Creek,	20 "
" 13 " " Butter Creek,	30 "
" 14 " " Umatilla River,	13 "
" 15 " " Camp up Umatilla River,	5 "
" 16 " " McKay's River,	16 "
" 17 " " Wild Horse Creek,	18 "
" 18 " Camp,	13 "
" 19 " Walla Walla,	9 "

up all stragglers and to keep in the rear of everything. The companies in front and rear alternated every day. Our transportation was limited to ten pack mules to each company, and one wagon to two companies. We had thirteen wagons in the train.

When about half way to Walla Walla, Colonel Steptoe, Captain Kirkham and Lieutenant Davidson passed us on their way to Walla Walla, with an escort of fifteen dragoons. Lieutenant Davidson goes up to take command of one of the Dragoon companies, in place of Lieutenant Gaston, who was killed in the late action.

During most of our march the weather was exceedingly hot. This was particularly the case the day we were obliged to advance thirty miles. It took the men exactly twelve hours, starting at half-past five in the morning. The sun—hot as the tropics—beat down on our heads with an intolerable glare, while there was nothing in the appearance of the country to afford any relief. Far as the eye could reach was only a sun-burnt plain, perfectly lifeless,—for the summer's sun, by burning up the herbage, had driven the game to seek refuge by the rivers. The prairie was covered with a miserable crop of salt week and wormwood, and even the horses of the officers drooped when the sun began sinking towards the west; still our camping-ground was not in sight. Yet, on the men marched, loaded with their equipments, and through a stifling dust, which added to the exhaustion of the heat.

The line of country through which we passed is varied, the plains generally barren and desolate, though sometimes covered with thick bunch grass which affords good pasturage to cattle. It is rolling in its character, and probably ill adapted for culture, except along the rivers. The absence of timber tends to give it a more waste appearance. Along John Day's river, (so called from a hunter who was one of the original members of Mr. Astor's enterprise,) there is but little wood, and that of a small size, often not larger than brushwood. Along the Umatilla and Walla Walla, on the contrary, the timber is abundant and heavy, and the water is excellent.

The valleys are the redeeming features of this country. The Des Chutes valley is admirable for grazing, as the temperature is such that cattle can be kept out the whole year and find subsistence. It is the place where formerly the Hudson Bay Company raised all the best horses they used. The Umatilla·valley is one of the richest and best adapted for cultivation of any on this side of the Rocky mountains. It has plenty of wood, and much of it is heavy timber. The Walla Walla valley, too, is a large and fertile one, and in places where cultivation has been attempted, it shows that the products will amply repay the laborer.

We saw no signs of Indians until the day before we reached Walla Walla, when before we broke up camp in the morning, two Indians (one a Walla Walla and the other a Cayuse,) came in, as they said, for protection. They told us that the Snakes and Cayuses had a fight two days before, and the latter had been defeated.

IV.

FORT WALLA WALLA.

CHAPTER IV.

FORT WALLA WALLA.

E reached Fort Walla Walla, July 19th, after a march of twelve and a half days. The fort is almost on the ground of the Walla Walla Council which I attended three years ago, when those tribes we are now to fight were all represented, and their great leader, Kamiaken, was himself present. It is in a beautiful spot of the Walla Walla valley, well wooded and with plenty of water. Ten miles distant is seen the range of the Blue mountains, forming the south-eastern boundary of the great plains along the Columbia, whose waters it divides from those of Lewis river. It stretches away along the horizon until it is lost in the dim distance, where the chain unites with the Snake River mountains.

At this post are stationed four companies of the First Dragoons, and two of the Ninth Infantry. The Dragoon officers are Major Grier, Lieutenants Davidson, Pender, Gregg and Wheeler. The Infantry officers are Colonel Steptoe, Captains Dent and Winder, Lieutenants Fleming and Harvie. Besides these, are Captain Kirkham, Quartermaster, and Dr. Randolph, Surgeon. The dragoon cantonment and the infantry post are about a mile apart, and we are encamped between them.

The two companies of the Fourth Infantry, which were

lately ordered up here, have had their orders changed and go to Simcoe. A command, consisting of three hundred men, leaves there on the 15th of next month for the Yakima country, under Major Garnett.

One of the first persons who came into camp to see us was a Cayuse Indian, Cutmouth John, who was Lieutenant Gracie's guide through this country three years ago, when I accompanied him on his march with a detachment of the Fourth Infantry, to act as escort to Governor Stevens at the Walla Walla council. This worthy had a dreadful distortion of visage, from having been shot in the mouth in a fight with the Snake Indians, and hence his *soubriquet*. He once lived with Dr. Whitman, physician to a Presbyterian mission which existed for a time near Walla Walla, and when the Doctor and his family (seven in number) were cut off in 1847, he defended them as long as possible and received at that time his wound.

John seemed very glad to see me, after our long separation, and during the expedition was a visitor almost every evening at our tent. He was exceedingly fond of talking about his former connection with the mission, and yet, it must be acknowledged that he had not retained much of the Christianity he learned while there. His sole stock consisted of two or three hymns, with which he always insisted upon favoring us, particularly when he had imbibed too much whiskey, a contingency occurring far more frequently than was for his good.

Colonel Wright, who is to take command of the expedition, has arrived, and drills and reviews are going on as usual. The Third Artillery drill twice a day in Light Infantry tactics, except Major Wyse's company, which practices at artillery drill, mounted battery, mules being used for horses.

August 1st.—Colonel Wright and staff this morning reviewed all the troops, each corps separately. The expedition will consist of about seven hundred men, while about a hundred will be left to garrison Fort Walla Walla, under Colonel Steptoe.

A few days ago sixty Nez Percés arrived, under an old chief, named Lawyer, whom I knew at the council in 1855. He has been a great warrior in his day, and is still suffering from a wound in his side which he received many years ago in a fight with their old hereditary enemies, the Blackfeet Indians. These are the most dangerous banditti among all the tribes,—perfect Ishmaelites,—who, while they are at war with all the neighboring savages, have nourished the most implacable hatred to the whites, since they first met them in the days of Lewis and Clarke. War is their employment, and the booty they gain by it, their support. They are admirable horsemen, and as much distinguished for their treachery as for their headlong courage. Their hunting-grounds extend from the Yellow Stone and Missouri rivers to the Rocky mountains.

The Nez Percé, or pierced-nose Indians, received this name from the early traders and trappers, but they call themselves by the name of Chipunnish. While they are the most friendly to the whites of any tribe in this region, they are at the same time one of the most numerous and powerful, roaming over the whole Rocky mountains, along the streams to the West, and across the almost limitless plains to the East, until they reach the hunting-grounds of the tribes of the Missouri. They hunt the elk, the white bear, the mountain sheep, and the buffalo, while they trap the beaver to sell the skins to the whites. They are celebrated for their droves of horses, which, after being branded, are turned loose to roam upon the fertile plains till needed by their owners: when this is the case, it requires but a few days to break them sufficiently to answer the purpose of their bold riders.

3

The warriors leave all labor to the women. They perform all the menial offices, arranging the lodge, cooking, and bringing wood; for it would be a disgrace to their lords to be seen engaged in these things. It would procure for them the title of *squaws*. Everything but the perils of war and the chase are beneath their attention. When at home and not occupied in preparing their arms, or in feats of horsemanship, they are gambling, lounging in groups on the mounds of the prairie, or listening to some story-teller, who recounts the exploits of the old warriors of the tribe.

The Nez Percés are blessed with a more tractable disposition than most of their brethren, and we have never seen any Indians who appear so willing to be instructed, not only in the arts of civilization, but also in the precepts of Christianity. At an early day the Presbyterian missionaries went among them, and their labors met with considerable success. A kind of Christianity was introduced among them, strangely altered, indeed, in many respects, to bring it into harmony with Indian thoughts and actions, yet still retaining many of the great truths of the faith. The Methodists subsequently added their teaching; and many of them have been brought into contact with the Jesuit Fathers, one of whose missions is established in the Cœur d'Alene country. We believe, therefore, that the theological creed of the Nez Percés, if now investigated, would probably be an odd system, which would startle an ordinary D. D.

Still, it exerted a very perceptible influence over their system of morality and their daily life. When with Lieutenant Gracie at the council, on this spot, in 1855, twenty-five hundred of the Nez Percés tribe were present; and as we were camped among them for three weeks, I had an opportunity of learning something of their habits. I found they had prayers in their lodges every morning and evening, service several times on Sunday,—and nothing could induce them on that day to engage in any trading.

On one occasion, at that time, visiting the old chief Lawyer in his lodge, on some evening in the middle of the week, I found him surrounded by his family, and reading a portion of the New Testament. On another occasion, on a Saturday evening, he was employed with a number of his tribe in singing sacred music to prepare for the worship of the morrow. The next day, therefore, we rode over to the Nez Percé camp, where we found they were holding service in one of the largest lodges. Two of the chiefs were officiating, one of them delivering an address, (taking the Ten Commandments for his text,) and at the end of each sentence the other chief would repeat it in a louder tone of voice. This is their invariable custom with all their speeches. Everything was conducted with the greatest propriety, and the singing, in which they all joined, had an exceedingly musical effect. We found indeed an odd mixture of this world and the next in some of the Nez Percés—an equal love of fighting and devotion—the wildest Indians' traits with a strictness in some religious rites, which might shame those "who profess and call themselves Christians."

Colonel Wright has had "a talk" with the deputation of the tribe, and made arrangements by which they have become our allies. This will have the effect of withdrawing some seventeen hundred Hudson Bay muskets from the ranks of the hostile Indians, though we understand there are some discontented lodges among the Nez Percés which will unite with them. Still, the great body of the tribe will probably be faithful to their pledge. A party, too, is to go with us to act as guides and scouts. At night they had a spirited war dance to celebrate the forming of this alliance.

V.

FORT TAYLOR.

CHAPTER V.

FORT TAYLOR.

AUGUST 5th.—To-day the Third Artillery received orders to march in two days as far as Snake river (about sixty miles), to erect fortifications. This will take about a week. By that time the rest of the command will arrive there, when we will all start together. For some days Lieutenant White has been employed in superintending the making of gabions for the field works, as there is no wood on Snake river adapted to this purpose.

August 7th.—We left Walla Walla at nine in the morning, and marched eight miles to Dry creek, finding the country covered with luxurious grass, and an abundance of wood and excellent water.

Our force, which is under the command of Captain Keyes, consists of one company of dragoons and six companies of artillery, with two twelve pounder howitzers and two six pounder guns. We transport with us, on pack mules and in wagons, thirty thousand rations.

August 8th.—Marched thirteen miles to Touché river, a well wooded stream, skirted by rich valleys, where the grass is too moist for the Indians to burn, as they have done that on the entire plains from Walla Walla to Snake river. They hope thus to drive us back, by depriving us of forage for our animals.

About half-way on our day's march an express arrived from Colonel Wright to Captain Keyes, with the information that the night before a party of Indians had driven off thirty-six oxen from Walla Walla, and ordering him to send Lieutenant Davidson, with his company of dragoons, in pursuit. Lieutenant G. H. Hill, (Third Artillery,) joined him in the expedition. After scouting over the country for thirty miles, as night approached, they had discovered no signs of the Indians, and being in a region with which their guides were unacquainted, they returned, reaching camp late in the evening.

August 9th.—Marched seven miles through clouds of dust, the grass in most places having been burned by the Indians. The country is so rough and broken that Captain Keyes was obliged to send ahead an officer with a party of men, to act as pioneers in constructing a road. In the course of the morning two of our wagons were overturned, but with very little damage.

An express came into camp in the evening, from Walla Walla, informing us that Lieutenant Gregg, with his company of dragoons, had pursued the Indians who had driven off the cattle, but only gained sight of them as they were crossing Snake river, and his command was not strong enough for him to venture over.

We ascertained there were parties of Indians hovering around us and in our rear, but we could not discover their strength. During the day we took prisoner a Walla Walla Indian, but no information could be gained from him, and in a couple of days he was released.

August 10th.—To-day we marched twelve miles, and encamped on the Tucanon, a narrow but in some places deep stream, and its valley fertile. It empties into Snake river, and somewhere in this vicinity we are to throw up the fortifications for our *dêpôt* while we are in the hostile country.

As soon as we arrived at camping ground, Captain Keyes sent Lieutenant Mullan, (Second Artillery,) who accompanies us as Acting Topographical Engineer to the command, with a detachment of dragoons, to find what kind of road there was to the river. He returned and made a very unfavorable report. At the same time, he decided that we were in the best place for the camp, as he had examined the Tucanon to its mouth, and the Snake river to the mouth of the Pelouze, to select the most favorable position for us.

We are now camped for a week at least, until the fortifications are thrown up, and Colonel Wright joins us with the rest of the command.

August 11*th*.—This morning Lieutenant Morgan and myself were detailed with a party of sixty men to cut a road to Snake river, which we accomplished by three o'clock in the afternoon. The command was then marched down and encamped on the river.

While working on the road, about half way to the river, we heard musket shots ahead, and thinking that the hostiles might have crossed the river and driven in our pickets, Lieutenant Morgan ordered me on with ten men to support them. On reaching the river, I found that some Indians had crossed to our side, and, on returning, had been exchanging shots with our sentinels. At the same time a small party appeared on the opposite bank, but a single volley from our men caused them to wheel their horses and ride off.

To-day Lieutenant Mullan had quite an adventure. Captain Keyes, with a detachment of dragoons, having gone to Snake river to select a site for the fort, while there captured two Indians, who were left under the charge of a sergeant and three men. They had not marched, however, a hundred yards, when the Indians broke from them and sprang into the river. The party fired at them without effect, as they were concealed by the growth of willows on the banks, which is dense and impenetrable, when Lieutenant Mullan dashed into the river to his waist, to secure one of whom he caught sight. The Indian was an exceedingly athletic savage, the sight of whose proportions would have

3*

tempered most persons' valor with discretion. But my gallant friend is not one to calculate odds in beginning a fight. The Indian dived as the lieutenant fired at him, and came up with some heavy stones, which, hurled at his antagonist, bruised him severely. He then seized Lieutenant Mullan's pistol, which had got thoroughly wet, and the struggle commenced in good earnest, grappling each other, now under water, now above. It might have fared badly with my spirited companion, but the Indian, stepping into a hole, got beyond his depth and was obliged to relinquish his hold, when he made off and escaped to the other side.

The working parties have commenced throwing up the field work, which yesterday, in General Orders, was named Fort Taylor, after Captain Taylor, of the dragoons, who was killed in Colonel Steptoe's fight. It is in latitude 46° 33′ North, longitude 118° 6′ West, at the junction of the Snake and Tucanon rivers. It stands at the mouth of a canon, with high bluffs of basalt on each side, about eight hundred yards apart; one being two hundred and sixty, the other three hundred and ten feet high. These, of course, command it, and with a civilized enemy we should be soon routed out. The Indians, however, are not scientific enough to give us any trouble in that way.

This spot seems to have been used as an old Indian burial-place, for we are surrounded by graves.

August 13*th.*—To-day a Roman Catholic priest, who belongs to the Mission in the Cœur d'Alene mountains, came to our camp. As the "black robes" can pass to and fro uninjured among the different tribes, he was sent by General Clarke to the Spokans and Cœur d'Alenes, to announce to them the terms on which he would make peace with them. The answer which they sent back to the General was exceedingly bold and insulting. They said,—"that the whites were always talking of war, and the first to propose peace; that the Indians were ready for war and did not wish peace, but a war of extermination." It is evident that their late success has rendered them perfectly defiant. They warn us, that if we cross Snake river, we shall none of us live to cross back. Dr. Perkins, who was at Fort Colville (the Hudson Bay Company's post) shortly after the battle with Colonel Steptoe's command, in his narrative says,—"The sword of poor Lieutenant Gaston was waved in my face by the Indian who had taken it from him at the time of Steptoe's defeat. The saddle of Captain Taylor was also shown to me, covered with his blood. These things the Indians displayed with exultation, saying that the white soldiers were women and could not fight, and the more that should be sent into that country the better they would like it, for they would kill them all. They seemed to be very much elated, and were confident that the United States troops could not stand before them. The old chiefs told us they were going to fight till they died; they had plenty of arms, ammunition, provisions, and everything they wanted; and when their ammunition gave out, they would poison their arrows and fight with them." Such is the temper of the enemy, to whom we are to teach a different lesson.

We have seen but little of the Indians for the last few days. Now and then they fire upon our sentinels, and shots are exchanged, but generally without effect. Last night, however, we had quite an excitement in the camp. About nine o'clock an Indian was heard shouting to us from the other side of the river. Captain Keyes, accompanied by the officer of the day and the interpreter, went down at once to ascertain what he wanted. On reaching the bank, the interpreter called to him, when he began cursing him in reply, and finished up by telling him that "he was a traitorous Boston (*i. e.* white) soldier, and had no business to be with us." As he ended, another Indian aimed and fired at our interpreter, when four of our sentinels at once returned the fire, with what effect the darkness prevented our seeing. The companies turned out at once, and remained under arms for about an hour; but the firing not being renewed, they were dismissed with orders to sleep on their arms.

August 18*th*.—An express was received last evening from Colonel Wright, saying that he would be here to-day, and the supply train the day after. This afternoon his command arrived. The dragoons and infantry are encamped about a mile from us.

The fortifications are nearly completed, so that in a few days we shall be able to cross. The works consist of a parallelogram, with two towers at diagonal corners. The Nez Percés tell us that the Indians are collected in large numbers at the Lakes, about five days' march from here, where they are going to meet us. We trust it is so, as it will give us an opportunity of finishing the war, instead of making it a campaign of guerrilla skirmishing in the mountains. For several nights we have seen the light of fires ahead, made probably by the Indians burning the plains to cut off our supply of forage.

As soon as we have crossed Snake river, the Indians will regard us as having "passed the Rubicon," and being in their territories. Then the campaign will begin in good earnest.

Our transportation consists of six mules to a company, and a mule to each officer, besides the three hundred and twenty-five mules which the quarter-master has in his train. Our entire train, therefore, consists of about four hundred mules. Baggage wagons cannot go beyond Snake river. We shall attempt to take only one light vehicle, which Lieutenant Mullan needs for his instruments.

Now as to our fighting force. The dragoons number one hundred and ninety,—the artillery, four hundred,—the infantry (as Rifle Brigade), ninety. Total, about six hundred and eighty soldiers, besides about two hundred *attachés*, as packers, wagon-masters, herders, &c.

Then we have thirty Nez Percés, and three chiefs, to act as scouts and guides. They were placed under the command of Lieutenant Mullan, but in an engagement he found their individuality developed so strongly that it was difficult for him to induce them to obey orders. Each one was fighting on his own responsibility. These, our allies, have been dressed in uniform, to distinguish them, during a fight, from the hostiles. Like all Indians, they are particularly delighted with their clothes, and no young officer just commissioned, thinks as much of his uniform as they do. They insist, indeed, upon having every minute portion, even to the glazed cap covers.

The manner of our march can be best shown by the two following Orders, which I copy :—

ORDERS } *Head-Quarters, Expedition against Northern Indians.*
No. 5. } *Camp near Fort Walla Walla.*
August 18th, 1858.

I. The residue of the troops for the Northern Expedition will march from Fort Walla Walla to-morrow, and unite with the advance at the Snake river.

II. Marching from Snake river, the order will be as follows :—
 1st. The Dragoons.
 2d. The Mountain Howitzer Company.
 3d. The Battalion of Artillery, serving as Infantry.
 4th. The Rifle Battalion of the Ninth Infantry.
 5th. Pack train of Corps and Head-Quarters.
 6th. One company of Infantry as rear guard.
 7th. General train of Quarter-master and Commissary.
 8th. One troop of Dragoons as rear guard.

III. The mounted troops will not precede the Howitzer Company more than four hundred yards; and on approaching canons or defiles, where Dragoons cannot operate on the flanks, they will be halted and the Rifles advanced.

IV. No fire-arms of any description will be discharged, either on the march or in camp, except in the line of duty, without the special authority of the commanding officer.

V. No person, except the employees of the Staff Department and the officers' servants, will be allowed to accompany the troops, or to encamp with them, without the written authority of the commanding officer.

VI. Habitually the Guard will consist of one company, and mount at retreat.

VII. It is announced for general information, that a body of friendly Nez Percés Indians have been engaged to serve with the troops. These Indians have been equipped in soldiers' clothing, in order to distinguish them from the hostiles. Company commanders will caution their men particularly in regard to these friendly Indians.

VIII. Whether in camp or on the march, the companies will parade with arms, at retreat and reveille roll calls, and the arms and ammunition will be inspected. The men will habitually wear and sleep in their belts.　　　　　　　　　　　　　(By order of Colonel Wright,)

P. A. Owen,
1st Lieut. 9th Inf., A. A. A. Gen.

(CIRCULAR.)　　　　　　　　　*Head-Quarters, Camp near Fort Taylor,*
August 24th, 1858.

The following regulations, in addition to those already published, will be strictly enforced on the march :—

1st. The mules with ammunition will be led, and follow close in rear of the column, in compact order under a guard.

2d. The baggage mules and supply train will be kept in close order in rear of the ammunition, and under the special orders of the Quartermaster.

3d. The ammunition for the Mountain Howitzers will follow close in rear of the guns.

4th. The animals for the Hospital Department will move with the ammunition.

5th. Particular attention will be given by company and battalion commanders, to see that the men, *at all times,* by day and by night, wear their belts; that their rifles are always at hand and in order; and that, on the march, the men keep in the ranks and in proper order.

6th. The camp signals will be sounded at the proper times, by the buglers of the Artillery Battalion, and repeated by the other corps. At retreat inspection, the last roll call for the day will be made at 8 P. M., a signal will be given for extinguishing lights, after which no noise or loud talking will be allowed.

7th. When the troops are to march, the company cooks will be called up in season to have breakfast ready immediately after reveille.

8th. Should the enemy be met while on the march, and a combat ensue, the entire pack train will be closed up, and either picketed or the animals tied together, and the whole enveloped by the rear-guard. In case of alarm at night, the companies on rear-guard the previous day will protect the train.

9th. The detachment of friendly Nez Percés, as well as the guides and interpreters, are placed under the special direction of Lieutenant Mullan, Acting Engineer, who will receive instruction in relation to their position, &c.

(By order of Colonel Wright,)
P. A. Owen,
1st Lieut. 9th Inf., A. A. A. Gen.

August 23*d.*—We were to have crossed the river at day-break this morning, but at reveille Colonel Wright sent an order that the troops should not move until further orders. The detention was caused by a violent wind and rain storm. Colonel Wright sent a wagon this morning back to Walla Walla for tents. Two evenings ago we had one of the most severe storms I have ever witnessed. It commenced about nine o'clock at night, and lasted until morning. The tents were blown down, and the boughs covering them scattered in every direction. The sand and dust were so thick that we could with difficulty see two feet ahead.

In the evening an express arrived, bringing the news from Major Garnett's column of the capture of a party of Indians, in effecting which Lieutenant J. K. Allen (Ninth Infantry,) was mortally wounded.

August 24*th.*—Still pouring in torrents, and our departure therefore postponed. At ten this morning an Indian boy was brought into camp by one of the pickets. Upon questioning him, he told so many different stories that we all came to the conclusion he was not what he represented himself, so he was confined in the guard tent. At one time, preparations were made to hang him, under the supposition that he was a spy; but the order was countermanded.

About the middle of the day we saw three Indians riding down to the bank on the opposite side of the river, waving a white flag. We sent a boat and brought over one of them, who was taken to Colonel Wright's tent, and questioned. He gave his name as Quil-quil-moses, and his story was, that he was a Spokan, living twenty-five miles this side of Colville, and had been told by the hostiles that he must join them, as the soldiers would kill him under any circumstances. Colonel Wright told him if he would come, with his women and children, and deliver up his arms, &c., he should not be harmed; but otherwise he should be shot, which would be the fate of every Indian taken with arms. He had with him another Spokan and a Pelouze Indian. After the "talk," he was sent over to the others who were waiting for him. His story may be true, but more probably it is devised to gain admittance to our camp. He told us, among other things, that the hostiles were encamped in strong force on the Spokan river, a few days' march ahead. This is in accordance with the news brought in by the Nez Percés scouts.

During the day two more boys were taken, one on the other side of the river, and one on this. One of them was driving a herd of about forty horses. We discovered that the boy taken early in the morning, and these two, were brothers, and had just escaped from the Spokans, carrying these horses off with them. Their father had been killed, and they taken prisoners, about five years ago. They were originally from the Yakima country.

August 25*th*.—The artillery began crossing at five o'clock this morning. Everything crossed over in the course of the day, except the dragoons and part of the quartermaster's train. It was amusing to see between three and four hundred animals swimming through the swift current, with Indians swimming after and driving them. The men and packs were crossed over in flat boats.

The horses taken yesterday, and the two eldest boys, were sent to Walla Walla, under charge of two Nez Percés. The other boy Lieutenant Mullan takes with him.

August 26*th*.—The dragoons crossed over this morning; also the rest of the supplies. Including dragoon horses and mules, we have about seven hundred animals belonging to the command. The artillery battalion was thoroughly inspected this morning by Captain Keyes, to see if we were ready for the field.

VI.

BATTLE OF THE FOUR

LAKES.

CHAPTER VI.

BATTLE OF THE FOUR LAKES.

AUGUST 27th.—To-day we left the river. We had reveille at half-past three in the morning, and marched at five. We made fifteen miles, and encamped on the Pelouze river.

August 28th.—We made but five miles to-day, encamping on Cheranna creek, where we found plenty of wood, fine grass and water. We are all on the alert, as any hour may find us in face of the enemy.

What the programme of the campaign is, none of us know. We suppose, indeed, that our commander can have no definite plan, as we are entering a country almost entirely unknown to us, but he will have to be guided by circumstances. An Indian war is a chapter of accidents. The camp talk is, that we have stores for only forty days, during which time we must find and beat the enemy.

August 29th.—Marched at six o'clock this morning, and made twenty miles, encamping on Cottonwood creek. The country hitherto has been rocky and mountainous, but to-day it became more level, and is thickly sprinkled with timber. It has however been hard marching for the men, the water being very scarce and poor when found. This evening we came in sight of the Cœur d'Alene mountains, and beyond them had a faint view of the Rocky mountains.

August 30th.—Left camp at six o'clock, and marched over a rocky, though for the most part level country. Water was found every five or six miles, but not good.

In three places where we halted for water, we saw the remains of Indian lodges. We made eighteen miles, to Camp Pedrigal.

To-day we first saw the Indians in any force. We had just got into camp when two of the Nez Percés rode in, announcing that a large body of Spokans were approaching. The dragoons at once saddled their horses and held them in readiness to mount at any moment. About half an hour afterwards shots were heard exchanged between the enemy and our advanced pickets. Two companies of dragoons were at once sent out, followed by the howitzer battery, two companies of artillery, and two of infantry. The rest of the command were left to guard the camp. We found however that the Indians had retreated before the dragoons, who followed them for some distance without being able to reach them. It was evidently a reconnaissance of scouts belonging to some large force in the neighborhood.

This afternoon two men of the artillery died from eating poisonous roots.

August 31*st.*—We left camp at eight o'clock, and marched eighteen miles through a rather level country. Most of our road lay through a cedar wood. On our right were hills running parallel to the wood, and beyond was a rolling country. We had not been out long when hostile Indians appeared on the hills. The Nez Percés rode in and reported to us, when Colonel Wright ordered the column to halt, the pack train to close up in our rear, and two companies of dragoons to deploy towards the enemy. In the mean time the Nez Percés had exchanged shots with them. They retreated as the dragoons approached them. In this way they accompanied us during the whole day, keeping at all times some distance beyond gun-shot. As we afterwards found, these small bodies were sent out to decoy our troops on and to deceive them as to the numbers of the enemy. They had chosen their ground ahead, in a strong position for attack, where the trail passes through a defile; and there they were awaiting the troops with their whole force.

Just before getting into camp, the hostile Indians rode up near our column, set fire to the grass, and fired upon our rear guard. Their object was to make an attack under cover of the smoke, but the grass was too green to burn freely, and the maneuvres of the troops at once defeated their intentions. As soon as the attack was made, Captain Keyes ordered me forward to report the fact to Colonel Wright, who, I found, had got into camp about half a mile in advance. Captain Keyes then ordered Captain Winder's company of rifles to deploy across the rear of the column, at right angles to Lieutenant Ihrie's deployed on the right and Captain Hardie's on the left, and parallel to the column, thus forming a rectangle about the train. The Indians retreated after firing, and took up their position on the hills on the right, overlooking our camp, where they remained until dark. We knew that their main body could not be far distant. The prompt movements of the troops on this occasion showed that they were prepared for any emergency.

We are now about twenty miles from Spokan river, and it is the intention of Colonel Wright to remain for a few days at this camp to allow the men and animals to recruit.

September 1st.—This morning, at daylight, we found the Indians, increased in number, still posted on the hills overlooking us. Their manner was defiant and insolent, and they seemed to be inviting an attack. At eight o'clock orders were issued to have the artillery battalion in readiness, as it might be called out at any moment. Shortly after, the dragoons, four companies of artillery, the howitzer battery under Lieutenant White, and the two companies of rifles, were ordered out to drive the Indians from the hill and engage the main body, which we ascertained was concentrated beyond it. They were formed into two columns,—one of dragoons, numbering one hundred,—the other of artillery and infantry, about two hundred and twenty strong.

One company of artillery under Lieutenants Gibson and Dandy, a detachment of dragoons, and the guard, consisting of about fifty men, under Lieutenant Lyon, officer of the guard, all under command of Captain Hardie, the field officer of the day, were left to defend the camp. As we did not know the strength of the enemy, and had four hundred mules and extensive stores, it became necessary to leave this force to guard the camp, lest it should be attacked in the absence of the main body.

After advancing about a mile and a half, we reached the hill and prepared to dislodge the enemy from it. Major Grier, with the dragoons, marched to the left, while the party of our Nez Percés, under the direction of Lieutenant Mullan, wound round the hill and ascended at the right. The main column came next, with Colonel Wright and staff at its head, followed by Captain Keyes, commanding the artillery, the third artillery, the rifles, and the howitzer battery.

As soon as the dragoons reached the top of the hill, they dismounted,—one half holding the horses and the others acting as skirmishers. After exchanging a volley with the Indians, they drove them off the hill and held it until the foot soldiers arrived. On our way up, Colonel Wright received a message from Major Grier, stating that the Indians were collected in large numbers, (about five hundred it was thought,) at the foot of the hill, apparently prepared to fight. Colonel Wright immediately advanced the battalion rapidly forward, ordering Captain Ord's company to the left to be deployed as skirmishers.

My place, as adjutant of the artillery battalion was, of course, with Captain Keyes. We rode to the top of the hill, when the whole scene lay before us like a splendid panorama. Below us lay "four lakes"—a large one at the foot of the barren hill on which we were, and just beyond it three smaller ones, surrounded by rugged rocks, and almost entirely fringed with pines. Between these lakes, and beyond them to the.north-west, stretched out a plain for miles, terminated by bare grassy hills, one succeeding another as far as the eye could reach. In the far distance was dimly seen a line of mountains covered with the black pine.

On the plain below us we saw the enemy. Every spot seemed alive with the wild warriors we had come so far to meet. They were in the pines on the edge of the lakes, in the ravines and gullies, on the opposite hillsides, and swarming over the plain. They seemed to cover the country for some two miles. Mounted on their fleet, hardy horses, the crowd swayed back and forth, brandishing their weapons, shouting their war cries, and keeping up a song of defiance. Most of them were armed with Hudson Bay muskets, while others had bows and arrows and long lances. They were in all the bravery of their war array, gaudily painted and decorated with their wild trappings. Their plumes fluttered above them, while below skins and trinkets and all kinds of fantastic embellishments flaunted in the sunshine. Their horses, too, were arrayed in the most glaring finery. Some were even painted, and with colors to form the greatest contrast; the white being smeared with crimson in fantastic figures, and the dark colored streaked with white clay. Beads and fringes of gaudy colors were hanging from their bridles, while the plumes of eagles' feathers, interwoven with the mane and tail, fluttered as the breeze swept over them, and completed their wild and fantastic appearance.

> "By heavens! it was a glorious sight to see
> The gay array of their wild chivalry."

But we had no time for mere admiration, for other work was in hand. Orders were at once issued for the artillery and infantry to be deployed as skirmishers and advance down the hill, driving the Indians before them from their coverts, until they reached the plain where the dragoons could act against them. At the same time Lieutenant White, with the howitzer battery, supported by Company A., under Lieutenant Tyler, and the rifles, was sent to the right to drive them out of the woods. The latter met with a vigorous resistance, but a few discharges of the howitzer, with their spirited attack, soon dislodged the enemy, and compelled them to take refuge on the hills.

In the meanwhile the companies moved down the hill with all the precision of a parade; and as we rode along the line, it was pleasant to see the enthusiasm of the men to get within reach of the enemy. As soon as they were within some six hundred yards, they opened their fire and delivered it steadily as they advanced. Our soldiers aimed regularly, though it was no easy task to hit their shifting marks. The Indians acted as skirmishers, advancing rapidly and delivering their fire, and then retreating again with a quickness and irregularity which rendered it difficult to reach them. They were wheeling and dashing about, always on the run, apparently each fighting on his own account.

But minnie balls and long range rifles were things with which now for the first time they were to be made acquainted. As the line advanced, first we saw one Indian reel in his saddle and fall,—then, two or three,—then, half a dozen. Then some horses would dash madly forward, showing that the balls were telling upon them. The instant, however, that the "braves" fell, they were seized by their companions and dragged to the rear, to be borne off. We saw one Indian leading off a horse with two of his dead companions tied on it.

But in a few minutes, as the line drew nearer, the fire became too heavy, and the whole array broke and fled towards the plain. This was the chance for which the dragoons had been impatiently waiting. As the line advanced they had followed on behind it, leading their horses. Now the order was given to mount, and they rode through the company intervals to the front. In an instant was heard the voice of Major Grier ringing over the plain, as he shouted—"Charge the rascals!" and on the dragoons went at headlong speed. Taylor's and Gaston's companies were there, burning for revenge, and soon they were on them. We saw the flash of their sabres as they cut them down. Lieutenant Davidson shot one warrior from his saddle as they charged up, and Lieutenant Gregg clove the skull of another. Yells and shrieks and uplifted hands were of no avail, as they rode over them. A number were left dead upon the ground, when once more the crowd broke and dashed forward to the hills. It was a race for life, as the flying warriors streamed out of the glens and ravines and over the open plain, and took refuge in the clumps of woods or on the rising ground.

Here they were secure from the dragoons. Had the latter been well mounted, they would have made a terrible slaughter. But their horses were too much worn out to allow them to reach the main body. For twenty-eight days they had been on their march, their horses saddled all day

4

and engaged in constant scouting,—at night picketed, with only a little grass after camping. They were obliged therefore to halt when they reached the hill-side, their horses being entirely blown.

Then the line of foot once more passed them and advanced, renewing their fire, and driving the Indians over the hills for about two miles. As we ascended, the men were so totally exhausted that many had fallen out of the ranks, and Captain Keyes was obliged to order a short halt to let them come up. When a portion had joined, we resumed our march.

The great mass of the Indians by this time had passed over the crest of the hill, and when we rode to the top but few of them were visible. Without again attempting to make any head, they had taken refuge in the woods and ravines, beyond the reach of the troops. A single group was seen at some distance, apparently left to watch us, but a shell fired from a howitzer by Lieutenant White, bursting over their heads, soon sent them to seek refuge in the ravines.

For a short time we remained on the hill, but no new demonstration having been made, Colonel Wright ordered the recall to be sounded, and we marched back to the camp. A number of our men had never before been under fire, but begrimed and weary as they were, we could see in their faces how much they enjoyed the excitement of the fight. Certainly none could evince finer discipline or behave more coolly. We had been absent from the camp about four hours, and had driven the enemy, from the point where the attack was first made, about three miles and a half.

As we rode back, we saw on the plain the evidences of the fight. In all directions were scattered the arms, muskets, quivers, bows and arrows, blankets, robes, &c., which had been thrown away by our flying enemies.   Horses too were roaming about, which our Indian allies were employed in catching.   It was amusing to see the troops returning with their trophies.   One officer had two buffalo robes and a blanket wrapped around himself and horse.

What the Indian loss was, we cannot exactly say, as they carry off their dead.   Some seventeen, however, were seen to be killed, while there must have been between forty and fifty wounded.   Among those killed, we subsequently ascertained, were a brother and brother-in-law of Gearry, the head chief of the Spokans.

Strange to say, not one of our men was injured.   One dragoon horse alone was wounded.   This was owing to the long range rifles now first used by our troops, and the discipline which enabled them so admirably to use them.   Had the men been armed with those formerly used, the result of the fight, as to the loss on our side, would have been far different, for the enemy outnumbered us, and had all the courage which we are accustomed to ascribe to Indian warriors.   But they were panic-struck by the effect of our fire at such great distances, and the steady advance of the troops, unchecked by the constant fire kept up by them.

The following is a list of the officers engaged in the fight.

FIELD AND STAFF.

COLONEL GEORGE WRIGHT, *Ninth Infantry.*

LIEUTENANT P. A. OWEN, *Ninth Infantry,* Acting Assistant Adjutant General.

CAPTAIN R. W. KIRKHAM, Quarter-master and Commissary.

Assistant Surgeon, J. F. HOWARD, ⎫
Assistant Surgeon, J. F. RANDOLPH, ⎬ Medical Department.

LIEUTENANT JOHN MULLAN, *Second Artillery,* Acting Topographical Engineer.

First Dragoons.

TROOP I.—Brevet Major Wm. N. Grier.
TROOP E.—Lieutenant Henry B. Davidson.
TROOP C.—Lieutenant Wm. D. Pender.
TROOP H.—Lieutenant David McM. Gregg.

Third Artillery.

Captain Erasmus D. Keyes, Commanding.
Captain E. O. C. Ord, Commanding Company.
Lieutenant Robert O. Tyler, Commanding Company.
Lieutenant James L. White, Commanding Howitzer Detachment.
Lieutenant Dunbar R. Ransom, Commanding Company.
Lieutenant George P. Ihrie, Commanding Company.
Lieutenant Michael R. Morgan.
Lieutenant James Howard.
Lieutenant Lawrence Kip, Adjutant of the Battalion.

Rifles.—Ninth Infantry.

Captain Frederick T. Dent, Commanding.
Captain Charles S. Winder, Commanding Company.
Lieutenant H. B. Fleming.
Captain J. A. Hardie, and Lieutenants Horatio G. Gibson, H. B. Lyon and George F. B. Dandy, were with the Companies left as guard to the camp.

After a while, our Indian allies began dropping in. They had followed the hostiles eight or ten miles, and returned loaded with their spoils, among which were some scalps. Foremost among them, as indeed he had been in the fight, was our friend Cutmouth John, waving a scalp, and catching up loose horses. Our allies concluded the day with a grand war dance about their camp fire, which was protracted far into the night.

VII.

BATTLE OF THE SPOKAN PLAINS.

CHAPTER VII.

BATTLE OF THE SPOKAN PLAINS.

FOR three days after our last fight we remained in camp, to recruit the animals of the command, exhausted by their long march. The Nez Percés were sent out to reconnoitre, but returned reporting no Indians to be in sight. During this time the weather entirely changed, growing damp and cold.

September 5th.—We left camp at six o'clock in the morning, and after marching about five miles, saw the enemy collecting in large bodies on our right. They rode along parallel to us for some time, all the while increasing in numbers and becoming bolder. We had just emerged from the rough broken country and entered on a prairie, when they were seen occupying the woods on the right side of us, evidently about to make an attack.

We had nearly reached the woods when they advanced in great force, and set fire to the dry grass of the prairie, so that the wind blowing high and against us, we were nearly enveloped by the flames., Under cover of the smoke, they formed round us in one-third of a circle, and poured in their fire upon us, apparently each one on his own account. The pack train immediately closed up, guarded by Captain Dent's company of rifles, a company of the Third Artillery under Lieutenants Ihrie and Howard, and Lieutenant Davidson's company of dragoons, while the command prepared to repulse the enemy.

It was curious to witness the scene,—the dust and smoke, and the noise and shouting of the Mexican muleteers driving forward to the centre four hundred overloaded animals, while the troops were formed about them with as much order and far greater rapidity than if no danger threatened. Then on the hills to our right, if we could have had time to have witnessed them, were feats of horsemanship which we have never seen equalled. The Indians would dash down a hill five hundred feet high and with a slope of forty-five degrees, at the most headlong speed, apparently with all the rapidity they could have used on level ground.

Four companies of the Third Artillery, under Captains Ord and Hardie, and Lieutenants Gibson and Tyler, were at once deployed on the right and left. The men, flushed with their last victory, dashed through the flames, charged and drove the enemy before them. As soon as they took refuge in the timber, the howitzer under Lieutenant White opened upon them with its shells. Then the foot charged them again, driving them from cover to cover, from behind the trees and rocks, and through the ravines and cañons, till the woods for more than four miles, which lately seemed perfectly alive with their yelling and shouting, were entirely cleared. Then they drove them over the rocks and scaled the walls of pedigal, dislodging them wherever they had collected. It was at this time that among those who fell was a chief, killed by Lieutenant Tyler's company, upon the saddle of whose horse was found the pistol used by Lieutenant Gaston, when killed in Colonel Steptoe's fight.

At length they were driven into the plain, when the dragoons under Major Grier and Lieutenant Pender, who had been slowly following the foot, rode through the intervals of the skirmishes, the charge sounded, and they swept the enemy before them. Among the incidents of the fight was one which happened to Lieutenant Pender. Firing his pistol as he charged, just as he dashed up to the side of an Indian he discovered that his revolver had caught on the lock and was useless. He had not time to draw his sabre, and was obliged, therefore, to close with his enemy. He grappled the Indian and hurled him from his horse, when a soldier behind dispatched him.

Yet our enemy could not thus leave the field, but groups gathered, and the flying stragglers again united in the woods which surrounded us on every side. Lieutenant Tyler's company was therefore ordered to sweep a hill to the right, while the companies of Captain Ord and Lieutenant Gibson charged the woods till they drove the enemy out, after a sharp contest. Towards the close of the engagement, Lieutenant Ihrie's company cleared a hill to the right and in advance of the column. A part of the troops then rejoined the column, flankers were thrown out, and the command continued to advance until we reached the Spokan river, where we encamped. Skirmishing continued all the way, the howitzer scattering the enemy whenever they collected in large numbers in the woods, and the foot soldiers then advancing and charging them. We had marched during the day twenty-five miles, the last fourteen miles fighting all the way. No water could be procured for the whole distance, and the men by the time they reached the river were entirely exhausted. Nothing kept them up but the excitement of the contest.

We have again had a proof of the efficiency of the new rifles, and the thorough discipline of the command, as but one man was slightly wounded.

Some five hundred Indians are supposed to have been

4*

engaged in the fight. How many were killed and wounded we cannot tell, from their custom,—which I have mentioned before,—of carrying off their dead at once. They were removed generally before the troops could cross the ravines to get at them. We learned afterwards that Kammiaken, the great war chief of the Yakimas, was almost killed. A shell bust in a tree near him, tearing off a branch which struck him on the head, inflicting a wound.

We discovered that some of the hostile Nez Percés were united with the enemy in this fight. A portion of the tribe has not acceded to the alliance which the rest have formed with us. The Indians apparently retreated but a few miles, as after dark we saw their camp fires in the distance, and also a great light which proved to be one of their villages they were burning.

September 6th.—We remained in our camp on Spokan-river to-day, to let the men and animals rest, and to have a reconnaisance made on the river. Indians were seen on the opposite side, and in the afternoon some few came over to our camp and professed friendship, showing us where we could find a good crossing.

September 7th.—Hearing that the enemy were in force above on the Spokan, we broke up our camp this morning at seven, and moved up the river about seven miles, when we again encamped. Most of our way lay through the wood skirting the river, the scenery around being very beautiful. Just before reaching our camping-ground, we passed the great Spokan falls. It is a high, narrow, basaltic cañon, where the whole river passes over an inclined ledge of rocks, with a fall of between forty and fifty feet. The view from every point is exceedingly picturesque. As high up as the falls, salmon are found in great abundance, while above them trout are very plenty.

Soon after leaving camp, we observed a small party of

Indians on the other side of the river, riding in the same direction with us. When we had marched about three miles, they stopped and had a talk across the narrow river, when we found one of them was Gearry, one of the head chiefs of the Spokans, who has received some education from the priests in the Red river country, and talks English tolerably well. He expressed a wish to have a "talk" with Colonel Wright, and was told by the Colonel to meet him at the ford two miles above the falls. It is evident their spirit is broken by the two lessons they have received.

Soon after we had halted at the ford, Gearry crossed over and came into camp. He said, "that he had always been opposed to fighting, but that the young men and many of the chiefs were against him, and he could not control them." This, we have reason to believe, is true; for Dr. Perkins, in his narrative from which I have already quoted, when at Fort Colville, attended the Spokan council, and makes the following mention of Gearry :—" He says 'his heart is undecided; he does not know which way to go; his friends are fighting the whites, and he does not like to join them; but, if he does not, they will kill him. During the whole time that we were in the council, Gearry never said a word, but merely looked on."

The "talk" administered by Colonel Wright, in reply to his excuses, was very plain, but by no means pleasing. It was thus :—" I have met you in two battles; you have been badly whipped; you have had several chiefs and many warriors killed or wounded; I have not lost a man or animal. I have a large force, and you, Spokans, Cœur d'Alenes, Pelouzes, and Pend d'Orcilles may unite, and I can defeat you as badly as before. I did not come into the country to ask you to make peace; I came here to fight. Now, when you are tired of war and ask for peace,

I will tell you what you must do. You must come to me with your arms, with your women and children, and everything you have, and lay them at my feet. You must put your faith in me and trust to my mercy. If you do this, I shall then tell you the terms upon which I will give you peace. If you do not do this, war will be made on you this year and the next, and until your nations shall be exterminated."

The Colonel ordered Gearry to communicate to all the Indians he should fall in with, what he had said, and also to tell them, if they did as he demanded, their lives should be spared. He also directed him to send a messenger at once to Moses and to Big Star, (other Spokan chiefs,) to bring in their people, and to return himself to-morrow with his people, at one hour after sunrise. All this he promised to do. Schroom, we hear, is at Gearry's lodge, and Kamiaken is believed to be not far off.

At noon, the son of Big Star came, in the name of his father, to ask for peace. After going into camp, nine warriors arrived to "talk" with Colonel Wright. He sent two over the river to bring in their arms, which they had left on the other side. After crossing, one mounted his horse and rode off, probably not having nerve enough to meet the Colonel again. The other returned, bringing the guns, which were found to be of British manufacture, marked *London*, 1847, and had evidently been purchased of the Hudson Bay Company, at Colville. Colonel Wright retained as hostages, their leader, who proved to be Pokantken, the head chief of the Spokans, who had been in the fight against Colonel Steptoe, and was the leader in the battles against us on the first and fifth, and also another Indian, who is believed to have been engaged in the murder of the miners in May last.

September 8th.—We left camp at sunrise, and marched

up the river on the Cœur d'Alene prairie. After advancing about ten miles, the Nez Percés (our usual scouts on the march,) came in to say they had discovered Indians on the right. At the same time we saw clouds of dust between us and the mountain, as if some large bodies were in motion. The column was halted, the train closed up in the rear, and the artillery companies of Captain Ord and Lieutenant Gibson, together with Lieutenant Gregg's company of dragoons, were left to guard it. The rest of the command then moved rapidly on, the dragoons under Major Grier at a trot.

We found it difficult to advance as fast as we wished, there being a very high hill to climb. The dragoons and Nez Percés, therefore, outstripped us, and we soon saw them passing over the hills. They had discovered that the Indians were driving off their stock to the mountains, which they had nearly reached. Our horsemen were obliged to dismount on account of the nature of the ground, and, after a sharp skirmish, succeeded in capturing the whole band, consisting of nine hundred horses. The Indians who had charge of them escaped to the mountains, after exchanging a few shots with the Nez Percés. These horses belonged to Tilkohitz, a Pelouze chief, and a notorious freebooter, who has stolen a large number of cattle, at different times, from the whites and from Walla Walla. They were captured near a wide lake, to the right of the great Cœur d'Alene trail, a place where large numbers of the four tribes winter. When the foot passed the first range of hills, they met the captured animals returning, under charge of Lieutenant Davidson, with his dragoons dismounted, and the Nez Percés.

When we resumed our march, as we had gone several miles out of our road, an express was sent to Captain Ord to march with his command and train along the river and join us. After a march of four miles, we reached Spokan river and encamped.

The Nez Percés having reported that there were some cattle on the prairie above us, and some lodges filled with wheat, after sundown, Colonel Wright dispatched two companies of artillery and one of dragoons, to burn the lodges and grain and drive in the cattle. They returned in the night, reporting that the cattle proved to be so wild that they could not be captured, but took to the mountains. The lodges were burned. We had marched to-day twenty miles.

In the evening, the case of our Pelouze prisoner was investigated, and it having been proved beyond doubt that he was engaged in the murder of the miners in May last, he was hung.

On leaving camp in the morning, we saw two Indians on the opposite bank of the river, who were watching our movements. During the morning they came down to the river, where the train and its guard were waiting for us, shouted over and demanded that the old Spokan chief whom we had detained should be sent back. The answer was a volley, wounding both of them, killing one horse and wounding the other. The Indians, however, both managed to escape. They were the sons of our Spokan prisoner, and one of them was in our camp yesterday, when his father was arrested. He then seemed very much excited, but we did not know of his relationship until he had gone.

September 9th.—This morning at daybreak, three companies of dragoons were sent out, and destroyed seven lodges used by the Indians as storehouses of wheat. Some were filled; from others the contents had been carried off and probably *cached.*

At nine o'clock, Colonel Wright convened a board of

officers to determine what should be done with the captured horses. They decided that one hundred and thirty
should be selected for our use, and the rest shot. It was a
disagreeable necessity, but one which could not be avoided.
Most of them being wild, they could not be taken with us
on our march, and must be prevented from falling again
into the hands of their former owners. Nothing can more
effectually cripple the Indians than to deprive them of
their animals.

Two companies were therefore ordered out to perform
this duty. A *corral* (enclosure) was first made, into which
they were all driven. Then, one by one, they were lassoed
and dragged out, and dispatched by a single shot. About
two hundred and seventy were killed in this way. The
colts were led out and knocked in the head. It was dis-
tressing during all the following night, to hear the cries of
the brood mares whose young had thus been taken from
them. On the following day, to avoid the slow process of
killing them separately, the companies were ordered to
fire volleys into the *corral*.

During the afternoon, our herders shot five of the wild
beef cattle on the plains.

In the evening, two Indians, one of whom claimed to
be a chief, came into camp with a white flag. They said
they came from Big Star, and belonged to his party,—that
he had started to overtake Colonel Wright, but found the
command had moved on, and as they had lost their horses
they were obliged to travel on foot. Colonel Wright told
them to remain in camp to-night and return early in the
morning to Big Star, to inform him that he should remain
where he was, and when we came near his village he
should come in with his women and families.

In all these offers of submission, we see the effect of the
last battle on the Spokan plains. Defeated in the open

country, at the Four Lakes, they determined to try it once more, where they had the shelter of the forests from which to annoy us. They had again the selection of their own ground; and this second lesson seems to have broken their spirit, and it is doubtful whether they can again make head with any force against us.

VIII.

THE CŒUR D'ALENE MIS-
SION.

CHAPTER VIII.

THE CŒUR D'ALENE MISSION.

EPTEMBER 10th.—This morning an Indian runner came in from the Cœur d'Alene mission, bringing a letter from Father Joset to Colonel Wright. Its import was, that the Indians were entirely prostrate and desired peace; and that they had requested him (the priest) to intercede for them. A few days' march will now bring us to the Mission.

To-day two companies more were detailed to shoot the rest of the horses. The officers and others selected theirs, about two hundred being saved in this way, and the remaining seven hundred shot. Most of those, however, which were retained, were shot afterwards, or escaped from us. They broke their fastenings or tore up the stakes to which they were tied at night, and dashed back again to their native wilds. They were entirely too wild to be of any use.

We learned subsequently, that nothing we had done so much prostrated the Indians as this destruction of their horses. At the time they were taken, there were some Indians witnessed it from the neighboring hills, who said, as we afterwards learned, "that it did not make a great deal of difference, as they would get them all back in a few days." Their plan would have been to *stampede* them, in doing which they probably would have run off our animals with them. They were therefore very much taken by surprise, when the next day they saw them killed. One of the Indians was watching us from the hill-top through a glass of one of the officers, which he had taken in Colonel Steptoe's fight, and which was afterwards returned to us at the Mission. Without horses these Indians are powerless.

September 11*th.*—We began crossing the Spokan river at five o'clock this morning. Each dragoon took a foot soldier behind him, and in this way we crossed in about an hour and a half. For a few miles our march was along the river and over the Spokan plains, when we entered the pine woods. We passed a small fall, above which the river is tranquil and sluggish, and there are indications of a lake being not far distant. After a march of fifteen miles through the pine forests, we reached the Cœur d'Alene lake, on the borders of which we encamped.

At noon, we came across four Indian lodges, filled with wheat, which we burned. Some *caches*, filled with dried cake and wild cherries, were also discovered and destroyed. This outbreak will bring upon the Indians a winter of great suffering, from the destruction of their stores.

Just before reaching our camping-ground, we passed an Indian burial-place. Each grave was covered with a low log house, surmounted by a cross. The house answers both as a monument, and a protection for the remains against the wild animals.

It is a peculiarity, we were told, about these Indians, that if one of their number is killed, his family have to decide the question, whether or not the tribe shall go to war. The chiefs have no voice in the matter. If the family decide for war, all the warriors have to go, as those who refuse are outlawed.

September 12*th.*—When we were about to leave camp this morning, Vincent, the head chief of the Cœur d'Alenes, rode in, bringing a pass from the priest, giving his name, and saying that he was on his way to bring the hostiles into the Mission.

All day we have toiled along, through beautiful scenery, yet a country difficult for a force to make its way, as our march has been through the forest in its primeval state. For the first few miles along the borders of the lake, the trees were scattered, but after leaving the shore the timber became so thick that the troops had to march in single file. At this point Lieutenant Mullan had to abandon his wagon, the only one with the command, and the howitzers had to be packed on mules and the limber abandoned. The forest seemed to become more dense as we advanced, until we could see nothing about us but high hills and deep caverns, with thick woods covering all, through which we wound our way in a twilight gloom.

This is a splendid country as a home for the Indians, and we cannot wonder that they are aroused when they think the white men are intruding on them. The Cœur d'Alene lake, one of the most beautiful I have ever seen, with water clear as crystal, is about fifteen miles in length, buried, as it were, in the Cœur d'Alene mountains, which rise around it on every side. The woods are full of berries, while in the Spokan river salmon abound below the falls, and trout above. In the winter season, deer and elk are found in the mountains. Many parts of the country are good for grazing, while there are a sufficient number of fertile spots where crops can easily be raised. When the Indian thinks of the hunting-grounds to which he is looking forward in the Spirit Land, we doubt whether he could imagine anything more in accordance with his taste than this reality.

At evening we encamped on Wolf's Lodge creek.

September 13*th.*—Our march all day over the Cœur d'Alene mountains was similar to that of yesterday. In some places the trail passed along the brink of precipices apparently a thousand feet in depth. The forest was so dense and full of fallen timber, that the pioneers had to be kept in advance, to cut with their axes a road for the animals. As seen from the tops of the mountains, when we crossed, the scenery was very grand, the densely covered hills, interspersed with lakes, rolling, as far as the eye could reach, to the horizon. Pleasing, however, as this might be to the lovers of the picturesque, the march, although only eighteen miles, was a very toilsome one to the men and animals. The rear guard did not reach camp till nine o'clock at night.

On these marches, the officers were mounted, and yet it was not so exclusive a privilege as might be supposed. When the march was long, and particularly during some of the excessively sultry weather, some of the men who were trudging along under the weight of their arms and equipments, would give out from exhaustion. Every little while one would fall out of the ranks. Then the surgeon stops, administers to him a restorative, and, as we had been obliged to abandon the hospital wagon on crossing Snake river, some officer dismounts and gives him his horse. So it often happened that we went on foot for half or even the whole of the day's march.

We first came in sight of the Cœur d'Alene mission when about five miles off. It is situated in a beautiful valley, surrounded by the Cœur d'Alene mountains. A pretty stream, a branch of the Cœur d'Alene river, with clear cold water, runs along side of it, furnishing means of irrigation. In the centre of the Mission stands the church, and round it cluster the other buildings,—a mill, a couple of houses for the priests, the dwellings of the Indian converts, and some barns to store their produce. We encamped about a quarter of a mile from it. The priests, in the evening, sent a wagon full of vegetables to the officers.

September 16*th.*—This morning, in company with several other officers, I visited the Mission. There are two priests, Fathers Joset and Minitre, with three lay brothers, attached to it, by whom we were received with great kindness and politeness, and all the information for which we asked, both with regard to their mission and the Indians, was readily given.

The Mission was established in 1846, and is an offshoot of the Mission of St. Joseph, about thirty miles from here. Their chapel is a prominent building, constructed of hewn timber, and mortar mixed with straw. It will hold about three hundred persons, but is still unfinished in the inside.

We found but about forty Indians living at the Mission, who are instructed and employed by the priests. With their own lodges and gardens about them, they appear to be perfectly happy and contented. There is no doubt but what the priests have had a most happy influence over them. Most of the tribe, it is true, in a moment of excitement, and, it is believed, in opposition to the priests, rushed into this war, yet generally they are easily managed, and no Indians with whom we have met have impressed us so favorably. And so it may continue to be while they are buried in these mountains. But as soon as the stream of population flows up to them, they will be contaminated by the vices of the white men, and their end will be that of every other tribe which has been brought into contact with civilization. At the same time, from their courage and the natural defences of their country, they can prove most dangerous enemies.

The priests told us that the Cœur d'Alenes cannot muster more than one hundred warriors, nor does the whole tribe contain more than four hundred souls. Most of them were engaged in the recent fights. The Spokans amount to about four times that number.

Had we delayed our coming a few days longer, the priests informed us, we should have found the Mission deserted, as they were ordered by their Superior to break it up, if the Indians went out to fight. They were about removing into the Blackfeet country. If the Indians come in and submit to the terms proposed, they will remain.

We learned too from them, that in one of the lodges burned by the dragoons the night we were on Spokan river, was the carriage belonging to one of the howitzers taken in the fight with Colonel Steptoe.

This afternoon Vincent returned and reported that the Cœur d'Alenes were afraid to come in; but since then some few have arrived. The priests will now be exceedingly useful to us. The Indians, terrified by the lessons they have had, although desirous of peace, seem afraid to come near the whites to sue for it. They are scattered, and hiding in the mountains and ravines, and it will be through the agency and influence of their priests alone, that we shall be able to reassure them and induce them to accede to the necessary terms.

September 15*th* —We are waiting for the Indians. Some Cœur d'Alenes came in to-day, and turned over to the quarter-master all the property in their possession taken in Colonel Steptoe's fight. It consisted of two horses, two mules, and a variety of small articles.

September 16*th.*—Our mail was sent out to-day in charge of four Cœur d'Alene Indian runners. We must take our risk of its reaching the settlements in safety, without being intercepted by Indian parties, or perhaps carried off by our new "mail agents."

Some few more Indians came in to-day. The old Spokan chief was released this morning and sent to the Mission. He promises to join his people and try to bring them in.

September 17*th.*—About a dozen Indians, with their families, came in this morning. Now that some have tried the experiment and find themselves unharmed, we may hope that the rest will follow their example. With some other officers I made a visit to the Mission, and then returned to attend the council.

IX.

THE CŒUR D'ALENE COUNCIL.

CHAPTER IX.

THE CŒUR D'ALENE COUNCIL.

HE Cœur d' Alenes have always been remarked for their determined opposition to the whites. They perseveringly set themselves against any intrusion into their country, and if they had possessed strength to carry out their wishes, their hunting-grounds would never have been trodden by the foot of a white man. It was from this trait that they received their name—Cœur d'Alene—pointed hearts, or hearts of arrows. They were now for the first time to meet the whites in council, where their only hope was in unqualified submission. It was the first meeting of the kind on our expedition, and we were now to witness the effect of the severe lesson which the Indians had been taught.

The council met in front of Colonel Wright's tent. A bower had been hastily constructed of branches of trees, and in this sylvan saloon we were to meet the sons of the forest. At one end was the Colonel, surrounded by his officers, while the rest of the space was filled by the Cœur d'Alenes, generally (as an Indian chief once expressed it) " resting on the bosom of their mother earth." About a hundred and fifty were present. Our two regular Interpreters were there, and also Father Joset from the Mission, who lent us his aid in interpreting to Vincent, when the latter repeated it to the other chiefs present.

The Council was opened by Vincent, the Cœur d'Alene chief, who addressed Colonel Wright thus:

" I have committed a great crime. I am fully conscious

of it, and am deeply sorry for it. I and all my people are rejoiced that you are willing to forgive us. I have done."

COLONEL WRIGHT. (To the Indians.) "As your chief has said, you have committed a great crime. It has angered your Great Father, and I have been sent to punish you. You attacked Colonel Steptoe when he was passing peaceably through your country, and you have killed some of his men. But you asked for peace, and you shall have it, on certain conditions.

"You see that you fight against us hopelessly. I have a great many soldiers. I have a great many men at Walla Walla, and have a large body coming from Salt Lake City. What can you do against us? I can place my soldiers on your plains, by your fishing-grounds, and in the mountains where you catch game, and your helpless families cannot run away.

"You shall have peace on the following conditions. You must deliver to me, to take to the General, the men who struck the first blow in the affair with Colonel Steptoe. You must deliver to me to take to Walla Walla, one chief and four warriors with their families. You must deliver up to me all property taken in the affair with Colonel Steptoe. You must allow all troops and other white men to pass unmolested through your country. You must not allow any hostile Indians to come into your country, and not engage in any hostilities against any white man. I promise you, that if you will comply with all my requirements, none of your people shall be harmed, but I will withdraw from your country and you shall have peace forever.

"I also require that the hatchet shall be buried between you and our friends, the Nez Percés."

The Nez Percés were called, and the part of the speech referring to them was repeated to the Cœur d'Alenes in their presence.

VINCENT replied:—"I desire to hear what the Nez Percés' heart is."

HAITZEMALIKEN, (the chief of the Nez Percés,) stood forth and said:—"You behold me before you, and I will lay my heart open to you. I desire there shall be peace between us. It shall be as the Colonel says. I will never wage war against any of the friends of the white man."

VINCENT. "It does my heart good and makes also my people glad, to hear you speak so. I have desired peace between us. There shall never be war between our people, nor between us and the white men. The past is forgotten."

The propositions of the Colonel were then formally accepted, and having been signed by him and his offcers, they were signed also by Vincent and the other chiefs and head men. They then smoked the pipe of peace all round, and the council broke up.

The old Spokan chief whom we formerly held as prisoner, was also there, and made a short speech, the import of which was, that he was also satisfied, and would go and try to bring in his people. He left the camp as soon as the council had adjourned.

Everything seems to be settling down on quite a pacific footing. The Indians, this afternoon, returned quite a number of things taken in the fight with Colonel Steptoe. Trading, too, goes on quite briskly. Blankets and shirts are exchanged for robes, moccasins, and arms. The Fathers send us vegetables every day, besides milk and butter; two luxuries which we have not seen for a long time.

To-day we noticed at the Mission a number of women, who were evidently in great distress and weeping bitterly. Some were mourning for those who had fallen in battle, and others for the hostages who were to be taken off by us.

The Indians seem amazed at our being so friendly with them, after their hostilities. Father Joset told them, as a solution of the matter, that "the soldiers were like lions in war and lambs in peace."

We find, from conversing with the Indians, what was the system of tactics they had arranged for the campaign. They expected to be attacked first by the dragoons, whom they intended to fight as they did Colonel Steptoe, and expected the same result. To this purpose they devoted their powder and ball. Having disposed of the dragoons, they would have the infantry in their power, cut off from all succour in the midst of a hostile country. They were then to keep riding round them, as they would have far outnumbered them, and shooting them with their arrows. They well knew, too, that their first success against our force would have doubled their numbers. Indian runners would at once have spread the news through the country, the wavering and undecided would have cast in their lot with them, warriors from the most distant tribes have hurried on to share in the spoil, and on both sides of the mountains we should have had on our hands a war of extermination against the whites.

The long range rifles upset this beautiful scheme. They expected, they told us, that as soon as the infantry fired they would retire and load again. They were very much surprised, therefore, to see them advance all the time, keeping up a steady and uninterrupted fire. They compared the soldiers to bears, that when they fired a shot, the soldiers advanced always to the spot where it fell instead of retiring.

We learned that, on our march to the Mission, a war-party of the Pelouzes were following in our rear, and when Lieutenant Mullan's wagon and the limber of the Howitzer battery were abandoned, they burned them.

September 18*th*.—This morning we resumed our march, and once more plunged into the wilderness. We have now reached the most distant point of our expedition, and begin our retrograde movement. It is the object of Col. Wright to look after the Spokans and other tribes, on his march down through the country. We left the Mission at seven o'clock, and after advancing about two miles, struck the Cœur d'Alene river, our way at first for a few miles passing through a thickly wooded country, and then over an open bottom running along the bank of the river. The

Cœur d'Alene is narrow and winding, and deep enough, it is said, for a line-of-battle ship, though not sufficiently wide.

Our march of the day was thirteen miles. Some of our hostages and guides went with us, while others came down the river in canoes and met us at our camp.

During the afternoon, one supply train, one company of dragoons, and the howitzer battery, crossed the river. They were taken over in two canvas boats belonging to the quarter-master, assisted by the Indians in their canoes.

September 19*th.*—This morning the rest of the command crossed the river. One dragoon horse and two mules were drowned in making the passage.

Sept. 20*th.*—Marched at six this morning. About a mile from the river we entered the thick timber, through which we toiled with great exertions for nine miles, until we emerged once more on the banks of the St. Joseph's river. After marching along its banks for about four miles, we encamped, having advanced thirteen miles, the greater part of the way through the dense forests. The St. Joseph's is a beautiful stream,—narrow and deep, and its banks lined with timber.

Had we been in a mood for the picturesque, we might have been delighted with the scenery through the day. The views from the mountains over which we passed, were most beautiful. At times, a large number of lakes, streams and ponds were in sight at once. Just before reaching the river, we passed the spot where the Mission of the Sacred Heart (to the Cœur d'Alenes,) formerly stood, before it was removed to its present location.

This evening the express came in with the mails, bringing us eighteen days later news from the regions of civilization. The rest of our hostages came in to-day, having been off to get their families and horses. They turned over to our quarter-master some horses and mules taken from Colonel Steptoe's command.

In the beginning of September, Donati's comet appeared, and night after night it has been streaming above us in all its glory. Strange as it may seem, it has exerted a powerful influence over the Indians, in our behalf. Appearing just as we entered the country, it seemed to them like some huge besom to sweep them from the earth. The effect was probably much increased by the fact, that it disappeared about the time our campaign ended and the treaties were formed. They must have imagined that it had been sent home to their Great Father in Washington, to be put away until required the next time.

September 21st.—Last evening the supply train was crossed over the river, and this morning the rest of the command made the passage. The Indians again did us good service in pointing out the ford, and in helping across the men and supplies. The whole command had reached the other side by one in the afternoon.

We crossed near a Cœur d'Alene village, which was the residence of one of the hostages who was to accompany us, and we witnessed his taking leave of his family. In bidding them farewell, he evidently could not repress his tears, and after looking back once more, by a great effort he tore himself away and hurried from the spot. It was a scene very different from the pictures of Mohegan indifference given by Fenimore Cooper.

Since granting peace to the Cœur d'Alenes, we have discovered, what we before suspected, that the discontented portion of the Nez Percés had joined the enemy, and were engaged in the two fights against us. The friendly Indians report there were about forty lodges.

As soon as we left the river, we entered the heavy timber, and after a march of about five miles reached a small stream where we were obliged to encamp, for the sake of the water, although it was scarce. In the afternoon a chief with ten "braves" came into the camp. They represented themselves as Nez Percés, though we found they in reality were Pelouzes. They said they had been in the two fights against us, but having heard that peace had been granted to the Cœur d'Alenes, they wished it extended to them also.

X.

THE SPOKAN COUNCIL.

CHAPTER X.

THE SPOKAN COUNCIL.

EPTEMBER 22d.—We left camp at half-past six this morning, and marched seventeen miles through a rolling country, occasionally diversified by open timber.

When we reached camp, we found that the head chiefs and warriors of the Spokans had come in, accompanied by Father Joset. Kamiaken and Tilkohitz were in last evening, but their courage seemed to have failed before the time of meeting Colonel Wright, and they went off again. Colonel Wright sent Gearry (the Spokan chief) and Big Star out after Kamiaken, telling him to come in and he should not be harmed; but if he did not surrender himself, he (the Colonel) would hunt him down until he captured him, and then put him to death.

Kamiaken has been for years the most powerful chief among all these tribes, and at the same time the most relentless enemy of the whites. He is the head chief of the Yakimas, his mother having been a Yakima, and his father a Pelouze. This gave him great influence with both these tribes, and by his talents he has acquired authority with all the northern Indian nations. He seems to occupy the same position with them that Tecumpsah formerly did with our north-western tribes.

My first acquaintance with him was at the Walla Walla Council, three years before. There, it was evident that he was the great impediment in the way of any cession of the Indian lands. While the other chiefs, one by one, came into the measure, and even Looking Glass, the war chief of the Nez Percés, at first entirely hostile, at last yielded to the force of some peculiar arguments which are equally potent with savages and white men, nothing could move Kamiaken. With more far-reaching wisdom than the rest, he probably saw that this surrender of their lands and intrusion of the white men, would be the final step in destroying the nation. Governor Stevens was unable to induce him to express any opinion, but he sat in gloomy silence. Several times, when the governor appealed to him with the inquiry,—"We would like to know what is the heart of Kamiaken,"—his only answer was,—"What have I to say!" He was the leader in the outbreak which took place shortly after, when Major Haller's force was defeated, and has been, we have no doubt, the moving spirit in arraying all these tribes against us this season, and bringing on this open warfare. It is not to be wondered at, therefore, that he is afraid to put himself in the power of the whites.

September 23*d.*—We did not move camp this morning, as it was the day appointed for the Council, which after breakfast assembled in front of Colonel Wright's tent. The Indians numbered one hundred and seven. Besides the Spokans, were Pend d'Orcilles, Colvilles, Iles des pierres, and delegates from other smaller tribes.

We heard to-day a fact, showing what will be the influence of our two fights even upon the Indian tribes which were not engaged in them. One of the chiefs of the Colville Indians, whose hunting-grounds are far north of the Cœur d'Alenes, just on the borders of the British possessions, told his tribe that he had heard a great deal about the soldiers, but never having seen them, he would go down and be a witness of the fight which they knew was at hand. So he joined the other tribes, and was present at the battle of the "Four Lakes." When the fight was over, he turned his horse and rode until he reached his own people. There he called his tribe together, and told them he had seen the soldiers, but never wished to see them again; that they stood as firm as the oaks when the Indians fired at them; that they could march faster and further in a day than horses; that their guns carried a mile, more than half way as far again as those of the Indians, and he ended by advising them always to remain friends with the whites.

The Spokans being assembled at the Council, Colonel Wright addressed them. He promised them peace on the same conditions he had imposed on the Cœur d'Alenes, and announced that he expected to see them come forward like men. The Cœur d'Alenes had done so, and were now the friends of the government. Besides, this was the last treaty which would be made, and he wished the friendly Nez Percés Indians to be included in it. The hostile Nez Percés, who had engaged in the war against us, he would have driven out of the Spokan country; that the government would make roads through their country, where and whenever it pleased, and the workmen employed on them must not be molested.

The SPOKAN CHIEF replied:—"I am sorry for what has been done, and glad of the opportunity now offered to make peace with our Great Father. We promise to obey and fulfil these terms in every point."

Another old SPOKAN CHIEF said:—"My heart is the same. I trust everybody is included in the Colonel's mercy."

COLONEL WRIGHT. "It embraces everybody, and those who go with me to Walla Walla as hostages for the good behavior of the nation shall not be hurt the least, but well taken care of until their safe return at the expiration of one year."

The treaty was then signed by all the chiefs present, on the part of the Spokans.

During the council, Gearry and Big Star returned, and reported that they had been hunting all night for Kamia-ken without success, when at daybreak they found him, and Schroom, his brother, on the other side of Spokan river. They were unable, however, to induce him to come in, as he said he was afraid he should be taken to Walla Walla.

The conditions of peace were then interpreted to these two chiefs, and the treaty signed by them.

Among those present at the council, was Milcapzy, a Cœur d'Alene chief, who was not at the treaty made with his own nation. As the council was closing, Colonel Wright singled him out and addressed him thus:—

"Milcapzy! I saw your letter to General Clarke. You say to the General,—'Perhaps you think that we are poor and want peace. We are neither poor nor do we want peace. If you want peace, you must come and ask for it. And take care that you do not come beyond the battle ground.'

"Who now asks for peace? I do not. And where stands the battle ground? Milcapzy thinks he is rich. He has bands of horses, and houses, and farms, and lodges full of grain. Let him remember that riches sometimes take wings and fly away. Tilkohitz* was rich once, but

---

* Tilkohitz was the owner of the nine hundred horses captured by us and shot, September 9th.

is poor now. Milcapzy! look upon the banks of the Spokan. I should like to hear Milcapzy speak."

Milcapzy reflected for a moment, spoke a few words to another warrior at his side, arranged his head-dress, and rising, said :—

"I am aware that I have committed a great crime. I am very sorry for it. My heart is cast down. But I have heard your talk just made in this council. I have confidence in what you say, and I thank you for it. I am ready to abide by the terms you propose."

The priest then explained to him the conditions on which peace had been granted to the Cœur d'Alenes, and he expressed his willingness to sign the treaty. The council was then dissolved.

Among the chiefs at this council, were Polatkin, the head chief of the Spokans, whom we formerly held as a prisoner, and released,—and one of his sons, the one who visited our camp on the Spokan the day his father was detained. His brother and himself were the Indians who were fired at by the guard, across the river, when demanding the release of the old chief. He is one of the most splendid looking men I have ever seen. He was shot in the arm below the elbow, and his brother was shot through the body. From what we could learn of him, he will probably not recover.

One of our hostages is Anthony, a Cœur d'Alene chief, who was in the fight with Colonel Steptoe. When Lieutenant Gaston fell, he took his body and covered it with leaves, intending afterwards to go back and bury him. When, however, he returned, he found the body had been removed.

XI.

OWHI AND QUALCHIEN.

CHAPTER XI.

OWHI AND QUALCHIEN.

THIS evening, Owhi, the brother-in-law of Kamiaken, came into camp, as he said, to make peace. I first saw him, as I did Kamiaken, three years ago at the Walla Walla council, where he opposed all treaties to cede their country, not only with great zeal but with much ability. His speech, of which I took notes at the time, particularly impressed me. It was thus :

" We are talking together, and the Great Spirit hears all that we say to-day. The Great Spirit gave us the land, and measured the land to us. This is the reason that I am afraid to say anything about this land. I am afraid of the laws of the Great Spirit. This is the reason of my heart being sad. This is the reason I cannot give you an answer. I am afraid of the Great Spirit. Shall I steal this land and sell it? or, what shall I do? This is the reason why my heart is sad. The Great Spirit made our friends, but the Great Spirit made *our* bodies from the earth, as if they were different from the whites. What shall I do? Shall I give the land which is a part of my body, and leave myself poor and destitute? Shall I say, I will give you my land? I cannot say so. I am afraid of the Great Spirit. I love my life. The reason why I do not give my land away is, I am afraid I shall be sent to hell. I love my friends.

I love my life. This is the reason why I do not give my land away. I have one word more to say. My people are far away. They do not know your words. This is the reason I cannot give you an answer. I show you my heart. This is all I have to say."

Defeated at the council, and the other chiefs agreeing to the cession of their lands, his next move was, in conjunction with his son Qualchien and Kamiaken, to organize the outbreak which took place the following winter. That was repressed, and now he has probably been one of the instigators of these last hostilities.

His greeting by Colonel Wright was stern, and the examination brief. A priest was sent for to act as interpreter, and give his answers. Colonel Wright had seen him three years before, in the former war, in the Yakima country, when he was treated with a leniency which, it was proved by the result, only emboldened him to further outrages. He then made pledges which he never fulfilled, and on this point he was taken to task. The Colonel has a peculiarly nervous way of putting questions.

COLONEL. " Where did he see me last?"

PRIEST. " He saw you in his country."

COLONEL. " Whereabout in his country?"

PRIEST. " On the Natchess river."

COLONEL. " What did he promise me at that time?"

Owhi looked exceedingly pale and confused.

PRIEST. "That he would come in with his people in some days."

COLONEL. " Why did he not do so? (*Aside.* Tell the officer of the guard to bring a file of his men; and Captain Kirkham, you will have some iron shackles made ready.")

Owhi hung his head and looked still more confused.

PRIEST. " He says, he did do so."

COLONEL. " Where is he from now?"

PRIEST. " From the mouth of the Spokan."

COLONEL. " How long has he been away from there?"

PRIEST. " Two days."

COLONEL. " Where is Qualchien?"

PRIEST. " At the mouth of the Spokan."

COLONEL. " Tell Owhi, that I will send a message to Qualchien. Tell him, he too shall send a message, and if Qualchien does not join me before I cross the Snake river, in four days, I will hang Owhi."

When this communication was made to him, he appeared to lose all power over himself. He sank on the ground, and the perspiration came out on him in large drops. He took out a book of prayers, and in much confusion turned over the leaves for a moment, looking at the pictures apparently without knowing what he was doing, and handed it to the priest who was standing by him. He was then taken off by the guard and put in irons. When the messenger went off, he said he did not think Qualchien would come in.

Owhi and his son Qualchien, are probably the two worst Indians this side of the Rocky mountains. The son is even more notorious than the father, and therefore Colonel Wright has been particularly anxious to secure him, He has kept the whole country, on both sides of the mountains, in confusion for years. They are Yakimas, but are in this country a great deal, where they have much influence with the surrounding tribes. They are both known to have been engaged in a number of murders. The coat Owhi wore when he came in, was recognized by one of our herders as belonging to a miner who was murdered last spring. The herder was with his party, but escaped.

During the evening a party of miners arrived from Colville. They brought very unfavorable news with regard to the Indians,—that they could not keep any cattle, for

they were at once stolen.   These Indians belong to small
bands, consisting principally of Okenagans, but including
renegades and outlawed Indians from every tribe.   They
would not attack a party of any size, but cut off stray individuals.   It is impossible, therefore, to bring them to a
fight, but they will have to be hunted down like bandits.

September 24th.—About twelve o'clock to-day, there trot-
ted out from a cañon near our camp two Indian braves and
a fine looking squaw.   The three rode abreast, and a little
way behind rode an Indian hunchback whom we had before seen in our camp.   The three principal personages
were gaily dressed, and had a most dashing air.   They
all had on a great deal of scarlet, and the squaw wore two
ornamental scarfs passing over the right shoulder and under the right arm.   She also carried, resting across in front
of her saddle, a long lance, the handle of which was completely wound with various colored beads, and from the
end of which depended two long tippets of beaver skins.
The two braves had rifles, and one, who was evidently the
leader of the party, carried an ornamented tomahawk.
With the utmost boldness they rode directly up to Colonel
Wright's tent.*

Captain Keyes, who was standing at the time in front
of the tent, pulled aside the opening, remarking, as he did
so:—"Colonel, we have distinguished visitors here!"   The
Colonel came out, and after a short conversation, to his surprise, recognized in the leader of the party, Qualchien,
the son of Owhi, and one of the most desperate murderers
on this coast.   For a few moments Qualchien stood talking
with Colonel Wright, with his rifle standing by his side.
His bearing was so defiant, that Captain Keyes, thinking

---

* For this description, as well as some other facts in this chapter, I am indebted to the notes of Captain Keyes.

he might meditate some desperate act, placed himself on his right, a little in the rear, with his eye fixed on Qualchien's rifle, ready to spring upon him on the slightest demonstration.

In a short time Colonel Wright mentioned Owhi's name. At this Qualchien started, and exclaimed,—" *Car?* where?' The Colonel answered,—" *Owhi, mittite yawa.* Owhi is over there!" When this was communicated, I was standing near him, and he seemed to be paralyzed. His whole expression changed as though he had been stunned. He gazed about him and repeated mechanically,—" *Owhi, mittite yawa! Owhi, mittite yawa!*" In a moment he made a motion as if he would use the rifle he held in his hand, and advanced toward his horse. He evidently saw at once that he had run into the toils of his enemies. The guard, however, had by this time arrived, and he was at once disarmed. On him was found a fine pistol, capped and loaded, and plenty of ammunition. Colonel Wright told him to go with the guard, to which he consented with silent reluctance, hanging back as he was pulled along, but evidently undecided what to do. He had not recovered from the stupifying effect of the news of his father's captivity.

Qualchien was finely shaped, with a broad chest and muscular limbs, and small hands and feet. When taken to the guard tent, it required six men to tie his hands and feet, so violent were his struggles, notwithstanding he had at the time, an unhealed wound through the lower part of his body.

In all the battles, forays, and disturbances in Washington Territory, Qualchien has been one of the leading spirits. The influence for evil which he exerted was probably greater even than that of either Owhi or Kamiaken. Of the three, he was the most addicted to fighting and bloodshed. He has been directly charged with the murder of nine white men at various times.   In the action of March 1st, 1856, on White river, Puget Sound District, in which Captain Keyes commanded, Qualchien was present with fifty Yakima warriors.   Of these seven were killed.   He went over the mountains,—he said,—"to learn to fight at night!"

Fifteen minutes after his capture, the officer of the day received an order from Colonel Wright, to have him hung immediately.   When his fate was made known to him, he began cursing Kamiaken.   A file of the guard at once marched him to a neighboring tree, where, on attempting to put the rope round his neck, the contest was again renewed.   Bound as his arms were, he fought and struggled till they were obliged to throw him down on his back to fix the noose, he shrieking all the while :—" *Copet six*— stop, my friends ; *Wake mameloose nika*,—do not kill me; *nika potlatch hiyou chickamen, hiyou knitan*,—I will give much money, a great many horses; *spore nika mama- loose, nika hiyou siwashe silex*,—if you kill me, a great many Indians will be angry ; *copet six*,—stop, my friends!" The rope was thrown over the limb of a tree, and he was run up.   Among those who assisted with great alacrity in hauling him up, were two miners, now in the quarter-mas- ter's employ, who had been with the party which was at- tacked by Qualchien and his band some months before. His last words, as the noose tightened, were a curse upon Kamiaken.

It is supposed from this, that he was sent by Kamiaken into the camp, as a spy, to ascertain what we would do, and he looked upon him, therefore, as the author of his death. He died like a coward, and very differently from the man- ner in which the Indians generally meet their fate.   So loud indeed were his cries, that they were heard by Owhi, who was confined not far from him.   The old chief, in disgust, disowned him, saying,—"He is not my son, but the son of Kamiaken,"—meaning, that he had followed the counsels of Kamiaken.

We have reason to believe there was some treachery in his coming in, for he had not met the messenger sent out to him, but had either come in of his own accord, or had been lured by the little imp of a hunchback, for some purpose of his own. His expression, especially that of his eyes, betokened a diabolical satisfaction. As soon as Qualchien was placed in charge of the guard, the hunchback galloped on to the upper end of the camp, where he related to his people with savage glee the part he had taken in guiding the chief to our quarters. So notorious, however, was the character of Qualchien, that his execution seems to meet with the unanimous approval of the Indians themselves. When informed of it, their first exclamation always is:—"It is right! It is right!"

The squaw proved to be his wife, the daughter of Polotkin. She was suffered to depart, and rode off with his companion.

It was reported next day in the camp, that Qualchien had a large sum of money concealed on his person. An order was therefore given to have him disinterred and examined, to prevent this from falling into the hands of the Indians. This was done, but nothing of any value was found upon him.

Is may be well here to anticipate in our narration, and give the fate of Owhi. After the execution of his son it was announced to him that he would be taken with the other prisoners and hostages to Walla Walla. He showed no signs of opposition to his being retained, but seemed to be contented with the arrangements made with regard to him. He therefore accompanied us on our march back to Fort Taylor, and crossed Snake river. Just afterwards,

6

however, about ten days after his son's death, one evening as we were crossing a small stream he became separated from the guard for a moment and left alone with Lieutenant Morgan, by whose side he was riding. Suddenly, he sprang from him and dashed into the thick underwood. Quick as thought, the Lieutenant's revolver was out, and he fired three shots, each taking effect, and wounding both Owhi and his horse. By this time, a private in the dragoons reached the spot, and gave Owhi the *coup de grace* by shooting him through the head. He died in about two hours.

Nothing has been done in this campaign so effectually to secure the future peace of the country, as the death of these two chiefs.

XII.

THE DEAD OF THE BATTLE
FIELD.

CHAPTER XII

WE are now only about ten miles from Colonel Steptoe's battle ground, and this morning a small force was dispatched to the place to try and recover the remains of the gallant men who were killed in that action, that with proper ceremonies their comrades may commit them to earth, paying to them the last honors which a soldier can have. They are also to search for the two howitzers which were *cached* in the neighborhood.

The party will be gone about two days, and consists of three companies of dragoons,—Major Grier's, Lieutenants Gregg's and Pender's,—together with Lieutenant White, with the howitzer mules, to bring in the guns. Dr. Randolph, who (as well as Lieutenant Gregg) was in the battle, accompanied the command. Lieutenant Howard was also with them, together with Lieutenant Mullan and his party. The latter, as Topographical Engineer, was sent to determine the position of the battle ground, while his assistants will make a map and sketches of the place. Some Spokans and Cœur d'Alenes went as guides.

To-day the Colonel had brought before him the Pelouze chief and ten warriors, who came into the camp on the 21st, representing themselves to be Nez Percés. They are such a worthless set, that there is no idea of treating them with the consideration shown to the other Indian tribes. The Colonel, therefore, told them,—"they had no business to fight against the soldiers, and he was going to punish them." He then put the chief and two others in irons, and told the rest to go and bring in their people, and if they did not deliver themselves up before he crossed Snake river, he would hang these three.

The rest of the Indians who had been in camp to attend the council, took their leave to-day and departed for their homes.

In the afternoon an express arrived from Lieutenant Mullan at Steptoe's battle ground, to inform Colonel Wright that they had been entirely successful in the object of their expedition.

September 25*th.*—This morning six or seven Walla Walla Indians came into camp. They said they had come from the camp of Kamiaken and Tilkohitz, that they had a letter from the priest, but it had been lost, and one of their number had gone back to look for it. They acknowledged having been in the recent fight against us. Being unarmed, the Colonel asked them where were their arms? They said they had left them at home. He then ordered two of their number to be put in irons, and dismissed the rest, telling them if they did not bring in their arms before night he would hang these two. One of them claimed to be related to Tilkohitz by marriage.

The miners from Colville left to-day. Their object in coming was to ask the Colonel to send troops up to their " diggings." But as they acknowledged the Indians would not fight, and were merely the thieving vagabonds of the different tribes, the soldiers could effect nothing. The miners must rely for their protection upon their own rifles and vigilance.

In the middle of the day, two Pelouze Indians came in bringing a letter from the priest. They were followed shortly after by seven or eight more. The whole party were at once taken to the guard-house and ironed. At evening they were brought up for examination, and being convicted of having been engaged in various atrocities, six of them were at once hung. One of them was proved to be the Indian who killed Sergeant Williams at Snake river, when, after being wounded in Colonel Steptoe's affair, he was trying to make his way back to Walla Walla.

At noon the dragoons returned from their expedition to the battle field. They reached there at twelve o'clock the day before, and found the hills which on that sad day were swarming with their excited foes, now as silent and deserted as a city of the dead. The whole battle field presented a scene of desolation. In the heat of battle but few of the bodies of the fallen could be recovered, and in the night, before their retreat, these were the only ones which could receive a hasty burial. The rest had to be left on the field where they met their fate. The wolves and the birds of prey had held their festival, and for nearly six months the sun and rain had bleached the whitened bones which were scattered around.

As Lieutenant Gregg and Dr. Randolph rode over the field, they could point out to the other officers the scene of each event in that day's hard fight,—where the battle began, where charge after charge was made to drive back the foes who so far outnumbered them, where Taylor and Gaston fell in the desperate attack at the head of their men, and where they were gathered in the night for the brief consultation, worn out with the contest, yet seventy-five miles of country to be passed over before they could place the river between them and their exulting enemies.

The remains of the two officers were found, and the

scattered bones of the men gathered up, to be brought back. The two howitzers were found, also, where they had been buried. The Indians had not disturbed them, but contented themselves with carrying off the gun carriages, which they afterwards burned.

One thing more remained to be done. Among the articles left on the ground was a pair of shafts belonging to one of the guns. These were taken and fashioned into a rude cross, which was set up in the midst of the battle field, to remind all future travellers of the sad event of which this had been the scene. And then, after depositing around it all that could be gathered up from the relics scattered over the hill-sides and wherever the fight was waged, they left the field in solemn silence.

Poor Gaston! my parting with him was at West Point, when full of life and spirits and bright anticipations of his future career. My last recollection of him, is in his grey Cadet uniform. I never saw him after, until I thus stood by his remains to-day. He was every inch a soldier; and when, during the last year, ill health weighed him down, and he feared the approach of that feebleness which would withdraw him from his duties, his military spirit seemed to be the strongest impulse he felt. He often expressed the hope that he might die in battle, and thus it was that his wish was gratified. He had a soldier's death, and will have a soldier's burial and grave,—

"The fresh turf, and not the feverish bed."

XIII.

THE PELOUZE COUNCIL.

CHAPTER XIII.

THE PELOUZE COUNCIL.

EPTEMBER 26th.—Left camp at half-past six this morning, and marched over a rolling, grazing country. By the side of a small cottonwood grove we saw the remains of thirty-four Indian lodges, probably deserted on the first advance of the troops into this country. Some of the lodge poles, from their magnitude, showed that the lodges must have been of considerable size. We marched fifteen miles and encamped on Silseepovestlem creek, where the water was good, but not plentiful. To-day was the coldest we have had on our march.

September 27th.—We broke up camp between six and seven in the morning, and marched ten miles. The day was exceedingly cold, and it rained hard all the time. The men, however, bore it cheerfully, for their faces were homeward, and in a few days they expect to reach Fort Taylor. For a few miles our way lay through the open timber, by the side of a large lake. We camped on a small stream.

September 28th.—Began our march at six o'clock this morning through a level, rocky country. We made about twenty-five miles during the day, finding water plentiful, our way, at one time, being along the banks of a lake. The grass for most of the distance of our route had been burned off. Through the whole day the weather was threatening, and before night the rain began pouring down. We encamped on a tributary of the Pelouze, about two miles above its junction.

Just before going into camp, we passed the grave of some distinguished Indian chief. It was large, covered with stones, and surrounded with a wooden paling. On a long stick, just within the paling, was a tin cup, and underneath was tied some horse hair. Outside the paling, from a pole supported by two other poles, was hanging the tail of a horse. It is a common custom among these Indians when a chief dies, to kill his favorite horse and bury him near him.

September 29*th.*—Moved from camp at six this morning, and after marching about two miles, struck the Pelouze river, along which we marched fifteen miles and encamped on its bank. Our march was over a rocky, hilly country. About an hour after leaving camp the express overtook us, bringing the mail. Our place of encamping seems to have been an old battle ground of the Indians, as arrow heads, and remains of other weapons, are scattered about.

A short time before reaching camp, a band of the Pelouze Indians, about nineteen in number, came in.

September 30*th.*—We did not march to-day. Early this morning a large number of the Pelouze Indians arrived with their families, and the Colonel determined, therefore, to hold the council. At ten o'clock the Indians assembled in front of his tent for their " talk." The Interpreter being present, Colonel Wright delivered to him the following complimentary and gratifying address, to be communicated to them :—

" Tell them they are a set of rascals, and deserve to be hung; that if I should hang them all, I should not do wrong. Tell them I have made a written treaty with the Cœur d'Alenes and the Spokans, but I will not make a written treaty with them; and if I catch one of them on the other side of Snake river, I will hang him. Tell them they shall not go into the Cœur d'Alene country, nor into the Spokan country, nor shall they allow the Walla Walla Indians to come into their country. If they behave themselves and do all that I direct them, I will make a written treaty with them next spring. If I do, there will be no more war between us. If they do not submit to these terms, I will make war on them; and if I come here again to war, I will hang them all, men, women, and children.

" Tell them that five moons ago two of their tribe killed some miners. The murderers must immediately be delivered up."

There was a brief consultation among the Indians, which resulted in one of them coming forward. He was at once bound, and turned over to the guard to be hung. The other had disappeared, to the evident annoyance of his countrymen.

COLONEL. " Tell them they must deliver up the six men who stole our beef cattle at Walla Walla."

This was at once assented to, and after another consultation the offenders were brought forward and immediately handed over to the guard.

COLONEL. " Tell them they must allow all white men to pass unmolested through their country, and must deliver up to me one chief and four warriors, with their families, to go with me to Walla Walla as hostages."

All these terms were at once agreed to, and the "talk" ended. Before, however, the council closed, four of the Indians,—the murderer, and three others who had been selected as notorious marauders,—were marched by the guard to a tree several hundred yards distant, and there hung.

XIV.

THE RETURN.

CHAPTER XIV.

THE RETURN.

OCTOBER 1st.—The artillery battalion, one troop of dragoons, the commissary and quarter-master's train, and the Indians and hostages under charge of Lieutenant Fleming, all under the command of Captain Keyes, left the camp on Pelouze river about six in the morning, and after marching eighteen miles, reached Snake river at noon and crossed over to Fort Taylor. We encamped on exactly the same ground we had occupied before the campaign. At the Fort, Major Wyse and Dr. Brown received us with the greatest hospitality.

October 2d.—This morning we took leave, with many regrets, of Lieutenants Mullan and Owen. The former is under orders for Fort Vancouver, and the latter for Fort Dalles, to resume his duties as Adjutant of the Ninth Infantry.

At noon, Colonel Wright, with the rest of the command, arrived at the river, and crossing over, encamped half a mile up the Tucanon. A salute was fired from Fort Taylor, in honor of Colonel Wright, as soon as he appeared on the opposite side.

October 3d.—Orders had been received for us to remain on Snake river, and we supposed, therefore, that for the present we had finished our march. Early this morning, however, an express arrived rescinding the former orders, and making Fort Vancouver the place of our destination.

The camp was therefore broken up, and we marched two miles and encamped on the Tucanon. In the afternoon Major Wyse joined us with his command, Fort Tay lor having been abandoned by the troops. It was left in charge of an old Pelouze chief, named Slaviarchy.

October 4th.—Left camp at half-past six this morning. Until eleven o'clock the weather was very cold and windy. It then moderated and changed to rain. The troops, however, made a long march of twenty-six miles, and encamped on Touché river.

October 5th.—We were on our march this morning, by six o'clock, through a country which was familiar to us. On reaching Dry creek, a distance of ten miles, the command was halted, and the pack train ordered to the rear. We then resumed our march and arrived at Fort Walla Walla at twelve, having been absent just sixty marching days.

The four companies of dragoons came first; then our thirty Nez Percés allies; then the hostages, drawn up in two ranks, under the command of Lieutenant Fleming; then the two rifle companies; then Major Wyse's company and battery of six pounders; then the howitzer battery, under Lieutenant White; and, lastly, the artillery battalion. By far the most conspicuous and *distingué* looking person in the command was Cutmouth John. He rode generally by the side of the Nez Percés, dressed in a red blanket, his head surmounted by a large skin cap, and holding in his hand a long pole, from the end of which dangled a scalp he had taken in the battle of the "Four Lakes."

The Inspector General, Colonel Mansfield, had arrived a few days before, and it was determined that he should exercise the duties of his office on the spot. As soon therefore as we reached the parade-ground, the column halted, the ranks opened, and Colonel Mansfield, with Colonel Wright and his staff, made a thorough inspection. There was nothing about the command, of the "pomp and circumstance of glorious war." During two months no one had slept under a roof, and all were begrimed with mud and rain and dust. The artillery and infantry wore blue flannel shirts drawn over their uniforms and belted at the waist; the dragoons had a similar dress of grey flannel. The officers had adopted the same, with slouched hats. The only marks of their rank were the shoulder-straps sewed on to the flannel. Yet all this was showing the reality of service. If there was little display of uniforms, the arms were in perfect order, and we believe the troops had never been in a higher state of discipline, or a more efficient condition for action. At all events, Colonel Mansfield expressed himself highly gratified with the result of his inspection.

After the troops were dismissed, we were most hospitably entertained by the officers of the post.

October 6th.—This morning notice was received from Colonel Wright, that all the officers should meet at Colonel Steptoe's quarters to pay their respects to the Inspector General. We met there at twelve o'clock, when a handsome collation was provided, and a couple of hours spent in pleasant intercourse.

October 7th.—To-day we turned to more solemn duties. At ten o'clock took place the burial of Captain Taylor, Lieutenant Gaston, and the remains of the men which had been found on Colonel Steptoe's battle-ground. It was from this post they had marched forth, and here they were to be laid to their rest. They were of course buried with military honors, the ceremony being invested with all the pageantry which was possible, to show respect to the memory of our gallant comrades. All the officers, thirty-nine in number, and the troops at the post, amounting to eight hundred, (reinforcements having arrived since our departure,) were present and took part in the ceremonies. The horses of the dead, draped in black, having on them the officers' swords and boots, were led behind the coffins. The remains were taken about half a mile from the post, and there interred. Three volleys were fired over them, and we left them where day after day the notes of the bugle will be borne over their graves, while we cherish their memories as those who laid down their young lives in the battle-field for their country.

———

With this scene this journal might fitly close. It began with the death of those whom we have now seen placed in a soldier's grave.

There was but one more incident connected with the campaign. Two days afterwards, Colonel Wright had a "talk" with the Walla Walla Indians. The tribe is one much reduced in numbers and importance since the pioneer trappers first came among them. They range through the valley for thirty miles, to old Fort Walla Walla, once a central trading post of the Hudson Bay Company, on the left bank of the Columbia river, near where the Walla Walla empties into it.

They have been exceedingly troublesome, and it was necessary to teach them a lesson. The colonel told them he knew that some of them had been engaged in the recent fights, and that every one who was in the two battles must stand up. Thirty-five stood up at once. From these the colonel selected four, who were known to have been engaged in several murders in the valley. One Indian, by the name of Wyecat, was particularly notorious. They were handed over to the guard and hung on the spot. I believe that sixteen of the Indians have been executed in this way.

On the 9th, the artillery battalion, under Captain Keyes, left Walla Walla, and after a march of eight days reached the Dalles. The distance being about a hundred and seventy-three miles, we have averaged twenty-two miles a day. It is exactly three months and nine days since we left there, and during that time we have marched seven hundred and sixty miles. On the 18th we reached Fort Vancouver, where we first landed in setting out on the campaign.

XV.

CONCLUSION.

CHAPTER XV.

CONCLUSION.

THE older officers regard the campaign we have just past through, as one remarkable in many respects.

One is, the little loss which has been sustained. But two men have died, and those from eating poisonous roots. But one man has been wounded in action; and we have lost, by all the difficulties of marching through the forests and crossing rivers, but three horses and about fifty mules. It is a proof of the skill and judgment with which the expedition has been conducted.

For our freedom from loss in the two battles, I have already stated we are indebted to the fine discipline of the men, the skill of the commanders, and to the long range of our rifles. Had we been armed with the old muskets, the result might have been very different. The whole campaign, indeed, would undoubtedly have ended, as it now has done, in the humbling of the Indian tribes, but we should probably have missed many from our ranks, when the column marched back to Walla Walla.

The object, too, was most thoroughly accomplished. The Indian tribes, hitherto so troublesome and defiant, have been entirely subjected. They have been taught the power of the government, their worst chiefs have been cut off, and hostages given sufficient to keep them in obedience. Of their head men who are hostile, none remain but Kamiaken, and Schroom, his brother. The former is reported to have fled into the Blackfeet country, and the latter is probably with him. They will certainly have no disposition to place themselves again in collision with the whites. It is probable, too, that among their own countrymen their influence and authority are gone. The tribes have suffered too much again to submit to their counsels.

That immense tract of splendid country over which we marched, is now opened to the white man, and the time is not far distant when settlers will begin to occupy it, and the farmer will discover that he can reap his harvest, and the miner explore its ores, without danger from their former savage foe. An Oregon paper, (and the newspapers are not accustomed to indulge in any unnecessary laudation of the Regular Army,) after the battle of the "Four Lakes," says :—"No event has ever done so much to secure the safety of our settlers as this victory. The people of this Territory owe a debt of gratitude to the officers and soldiers under Colonel Wright."

For this success, we are indebted to the energetic measures of General Clarke, concentrating at once, even from the banks of the Colorado, so strong a force in the country of the hostile Indians, and mapping out the campaign, the result of which proved the foresight and wisdom by which it was dictated.

For the conduct of the column when once it was on its march, none could have won "golden opinions" more thoroughly than Colonel Wright. Entering an unknown country, everything depended on his energy and talents. Of these I need say nothing, for they are shown in the history of our march, the arrangement of the two battles, the decision with which the Indian Councils were conducted, and the entire success with which all was crowned.

I might speak of the gallantry of my comrades, but this is recorded in the official reports of their superior officers. But none who had an opportunity of witnessing these battles, and seeing the steady advance of the Third Artillery and Rifles, as they drove the enemy on, mile after mile, from point to point, the gallant charges made by the Dragoons under Major Grier, and the conduct of the Howitzer Battery under Lieutenant White, can forget the admiration they felt at the perfect manner in which all was accomplished.

In our own battalion,—the Third Artillery,—but few of the men had ever before been under fire, yet no veterans could have shown greater coolness. This was the result of discipline, for which they were indebted to the untiring energy of our Commander, Captain (now Major) Keyes. Through his exertions the battalion had been brought to the highest point of discipline; and in the hour of battle, by his presence everywhere at the right moment, he contributed materially to secure the victory.

The column has now been scattered, and the officers have been dispersed to their different posts, yet they all look back with pleasure to this campaign, when they remember the unity of feeling by which it was marked. Seldom, indeed, has an expedition been undertaken, the recollection of which is invested with so much that is agreeable, as that against the NORTHERN INDIANS.

APPENDIX.

I.

OFFICIAL REPORT OF COLONEL WRIGHT,

AFTER THE BATTLE OF THE "FOUR LAKES."

Head Quarters, Expedition against Northern Indians, Camp at "Four Lakes," W. T.

Lat. 47″ 32 north. Long. 117″ 39 west.

September 2d, 1858.

Sir :—

I have the honor to submit the following Report of the battle of the "Four Lakes," fought and won, by the troops under my command, on the 1st inst. Our enemies were the Spokan, Cœur d'Alene, and Pelouze Indians.

Early in the morning of the 1st, I observed the Indians collecting on the summit of a high hill, about two miles distant, and I immediately ordered the troops under arms, with a view of driving the enemy from his position, and making a a reconnaissance of the country in advance. At half-past 9 A. M. I marched from my camp with two squadrons of the 1st dragoons, commanded by Brevet Major W. N. Grier, four companies of the third artillery, armed with rifle muskets, commanded by Capt. E. D. Keyes; and the rifle battalion of two companies of the 9th infantry, commanded by Capt. F. T. Dent ; also one mountain howitzer, under command of Lieut. J. L. White, 3rd artillery, and thirty friendly Nez Percés Indian allies, under command of Lieut. John Mullan, 2nd artillery. I left in camp all the equipage and supplies, strongly guarded by company "M," 3rd artillery, commanded by Lieuts. H. G. Gibson and G. B. Dandy, one mountain howitzer manned, and in addition a guard of fifty-four men under Lieut. H. B. Lyon, the whole commanded by Captain J. A. Hardie, the Field officer of the day.

I ordered Brevet Major Grier to advance to the north and east, around the base of the hill occupied by the Indians, with a view to intercept their retreat when driven from the summit by the foot troops. I marched with the artillery and rifle battalion and Nez Percés to the right of the hill, in order to gain a position where the ascent was more easy, and also to push the Indians in the direction of the dragoons. Arriving within 600 yards of the Indians, I ordered Captain Keyes to advance a company of his battalion deployed, and drive the Indians from the hill. This service was gallantly accomplished by Captain Ord and Lieutenant Morgan, with Company "K," 3rd artillery, in coöperation with the 2nd squadron of dragoons under Lieutenant Davidson; the Indians were driven to the foot of the hill, and there rallied under cover of ravines, trees and bushes.

On reaching the crest of the hill I saw at once that the Indians were determined to measure their strength with us, showing no disposition to avoid a combat, and firmly maintaining their position at the base of the hill, keeping up a constant fire upon the two squadrons of dragoons, who were awaiting the arrival of the foot troops. In front of us lay a vast plain, with some 4 or 500 mounted warriors, rushing to and fro, wild with excitement, and apparently eager for the fray; to the right, at the foot of the hill, in the pine forest, the Indians were also seen in large numbers.

With all I have described, in plain view, a tyro in the art of war could not have hesitated a moment as to the plan of battle.

Captain Keyes, with two companies of his battalion, commanded by Lieutenants Ransom and Ihrie, with Lieutenant Howard, was ordered to deploy along the crest of the hill, in rear of the dragoons, and facing the plain. The rifle battalion under Captain Dent, composed of two companies of the 9th Infantry under Captain Winder and Lieutenant Fleming, was ordered to move to the right and deploy in front of the pine forest; and the howitzer under Lieutenant White, supported by a company of artillery under Lieutenant Tyler, was advanced to a lower plateau, in order to gain a position where it could be fired with effect.

In five minutes the troops were deployed, I ordered the advance. Captain Keyes moved steadily down the long slope, passed the dragoons, and opened a sharp, well-directed fire, which drove the Indians to the plains and pine forest. At the same time Captain Dent with the rifle battalion, Lieutenant White with the howitzer, and Lieutenant Tyler with his company, were hotly engaged with the Indians in the pine forest, constantly increasing by fugitives from the left.

Captain Keyes continued to advance, the Indians retiring

slowly; Major Grier, with both squadrons, quietly leading his horses in the rear. At a signal they mount, they rush with lightning speed through the intervals of skirmishers, and charge the Indians on the plain, overwhelm them entirely, kill many, defeat and disperse them all, and in five minutes not a hostile Indian was to be seen on the plain. While this scene was enacting, Dent, Winder, and Fleming, with the rifle battalion, and Tyler and White with Company " A" and the howitzer, had pushed rapidly forward and driven the Indians out of the forest beyond view.

After the charge of the dragoons, and pursuit for over a mile on the hills, they were halted, their horses being completely exhausted, and the foot troops again passed them about a thousand yards; but finding only a few Indians, in front of us, on remote hill-tops, I would not pursue them with my tired soldiers; a couple of shots from the howitzer sent them out of sight. The battle was won. I sounded the recall, assembled the troops, and returned to our camp at 2 P. M.

It affords me the highest gratification to report, that we did not lose a man either killed or wounded during the action, attributable, I doubt not, in a great measure, to the fact that our long range rifles can reach the enemy, where he cannot reach us.

The enemy lost some eighteen or twenty men killed, and many wounded.

I take great pleasure in commending to the Department the coolness and gallantry displayed by every officer and soldier engaged in this battle.

1st. Brevet Major Grier conducted his squadrons with great skill, and at the decisive moment, after Captain Keyes had driven the Indians to the plain, made the most brilliant, gallant, and successful charge I have ever beheld. The Major commends particularly the coolness and gallantry of Lieutenants Davidson, Pender, and Gregg, each in command of a troop, for the handsome and skilful manner in which they brought their men into and conducted them through the fight.

The Major also speaks in the highest terms of Assistant Surgeon Randolph, who was with the 2nd squadron during the action, exhibiting great coolness and courage, and ever ready to attend to his professional duties.

Major Grier also reports the following named men of his squadrons, as having been mentioned by their company commanders for distinguished conduct.

"C" Troop, 1st Dragoons.

1st Sergeant James A. Hall; Sergeants Bernard Korton, and Patrick Byrne; Bugler Robert A. Magan; and privates James Kearney and Michael Meara.

"E" Troop, 1st Dragoons.

1st Sergeant C. Goetz; Sergeant J. F. Maguire; and privates J. G. Trimbell, J. Buckley, Wm. Ramage and F. W. Smith.

"H" Troop, 1st Dragoons.

1st Sergeant E. Ball; Sergeant M. M. Walker; and Bugler Jacob Muller.

"J" Troop, 1st Dragoons.

1st Sergeant W. H. Ingerton; and Sergeant Wm. Dean.

Lieutenant Davidson reports of 1st Sergeant E. Ball, " I saw him charge upon some Indians, unhorse one of them, dismount himself, and kill him."

2nd. Captain E. D. Keyes, commanding the 3rd Artillery, brought his battalion into action with great skill, and after deploying, made a gallant and successful charge in advance of the dragoons, driving the Indians from the hill-sides far into the plain; and again, after the dragoon charge, Captain Keyes pushed vigorously forward in pursuit as long as an enemy was to be seen.

Captain Keyes reports the gallantry of the officers and men of his battalion as admirable, and so uniform among the officers, that he cannot attempt to discriminate; the position of some of the officers, however, brought their conduct under the special notice of the Captain, and in that connection he mentions Lieutenants Tyler, White, and Ihrie. The Captain also says,—" The activity and intelligence displayed by Lieutenant Kip, Adjutant of the battalion, in transmitting my orders to all parts of the line, were most commendable."

3rd. Captain F. T. Dent, commanding the rifles, composed of two Companies " B" and " E," 9th Infantry, with Captain Winder and Lieutenant Fleming, brought his battalion into action with great spirit, and after deploying on the hill in front of the pine forest, dashed gallantly forward, and sweeping through the woods, drove the Indians before him, and came out on the plain, forming the right wing of the whole line of foot troops.

Captain Dent speaks in high terms of Captian Winder and Lieutenant Fleming, and the men of both companies, for the intelligent and fearless manner in which they behaved throughout the battle, and further says, " I feel I have a right to be proud of my battalion."

4th. Lieutenant John Mullan, 2nd Artillery, Top. Engr., and commanding the friendly Nez Percé Indians, moved gallantly forward in advance, and to the right of the foot troops, in the early part of the action, giving and receiving from the enemy a volley as he skirted the brush to the east of the main hill.

Lieutenant Mullan speaks in glowing terms of the Nez Percés throughout the action, at one time charging the enemy lurking in the brush and timber on the Spokan plain, driving him out, and pursuing him beyond view; and again a small party under the chief Hutis-e-mah-li-kaw, and Captain John, met and engaged the enemy, that were endeavoring to attack our rear; recapturing a horse left by an officer, while moving over the rocks and ravines.

Lieutenant Mullan expresses his approbation of the good conduct generally of this band of friendly Nez Percés, and mentions Hutis-e-mah-li-kaw, Captain John, Edward, and We-ash-kot, as worthy of special notice for their bravery.

5th. It affords me additional pleasure to present to the Department, the gentleman on my staff—

1st Lieutenant P. A. Owen, 9th Inf. Acting Assist. Adjt. General.

1st Lieutenant J. Mullan, 2nd Arty. Engineer officer.

Captain R. W. Kirkham, Assist. Quar. Master.

Assist. Surg. J. F. Hammond, Chief of the Med. Dept.

These gentlemen were with me on the field, cool and collected, ever ready to convey my orders to every part of the line, or to attend to their professional duties as circumstances might require.

Their good conduct and gallantry commend them to the Dept. Inclosed herewith is a topographical sketch of the battle field, prepared by Lieut. Mullan, illustrating the tactical part of this Report.

Very respectfully your obt. servt.

G. WRIGHT, Col. 9th Inf'y Commanding.

MAJOR W. W. MACKALL, Assist. Adjt. Gen.

Head Quar. Dept. of the Pacific,
Fort Vancouver, W. T.

OFFICIAL REPORT OF COLONEL WRIGHT.

Head Quarters, Expedition against Northern Indians,
Camp on Spokan River, W. T., 1½ miles below the Falls.
September 6, 1858.

To MAJ. W. MACKALL, Assistant Adj't. General U. S. Army :—
Sir :—I have the honor to submit the following report of the battle of the Spokan Indians fought by the troops under my command on the 5th inst. Our enemies were the Spokans, Cœur d'Alenes, Pelouses and Pend d'Oreilles, numbering from five to seven hundred warriors.

Leaving my camp at the "Four Lakes" at 6½ A. M. on the 5th, our route lay along the margin of a lake for about three miles, and thence for two miles over a broken country thinly scattered with pines, when emerging on to the open prairie, the hostile Indians were discovered about three miles to our right and in advance, moving rapidly along the skirt of the woods, and apparently with a view of intercepting our line of march before we should reach the timbers. After halting and closing up our long pack train, I moved forward, and soon found that the Indians were setting fire to the grass at various points in front and on my right flank. Capt. Keyes was now directed to advance three of his companies, deployed as skirmishers, to the front and right. This order was promptly obeyed, and Capt. Ord with Company K, Lieut. Gibson with Company M, and Lieut. Tyler with Company A, 3d Artillery, were thrown forward. At the same time Capt. Hardie, Company G, 3d Artillery, was deployed to the left, and the howitzer under Lieut. White, supported by Company E, 9th Infantry, were advanced to the line of skirmishers. The firing now became brisk on both sides, the Indians attacking us in front and on both flanks. The fires on the prairie nearly enveloped us, and were rapidly approaching our troops and the pack train. Not a moment was to be lost. I ordered

the advance. The skirmishers,* the howitzer, and the 1st
squadron of Dragoons under Major Grier, dashed gallantly
through the roaring flames, and the Indians were driven to
seek shelter in the forest and rocks. As soon as a suitable
position could be obtained, the howitzer under White opened
fire with shell. The Indians were again routed from their
cover, closely pursued by our skirmishers, and followed by
Grier, with his squadron leading.

All this time our pack train was concentrated as much as
possible, and guarded by Capt. Dent, 9th Infantry, with his
Co. B, Lieut. Davidson, 1st Dragoons, with his Company E,
and Lieut. Ihrie, 3d Artillery, with his Company B, advancing.
The trail bore off to the right, which threw Ord and Tyler
with their skirmishers to the left. A heavy body of Indians
had concentrated on our left, when our whole line moved
quickly forward, and the firing became general throughout
the front, occupied by Ord, Hardie and Tyler, and the howitzer under White, supported by Winder, with Gregg's
troop of Dragoons following in rear, waiting for a favorable opportunity to make a dash. At the same time, Gibson,
with Company M, 3d Artillery, drove the Indians on the
right front; an open plain here intervening, Major Grier
passed the skirmishers with his own and Lieutenant Pender's
troop, and charged the Indians, killing two and wounding
three. Our whole line and train advanced steadily, driving
the Indians over rocks and through ravines. Our point of
direction having been changed to the right, Captain Ord
found himself alone with his company, on the extreme left
of the skirmishers, and opposed by a large body of the enemy. They were gallantly charged by Captain Ord, and
driven successfully from the high table rocks where they had
taken refuge. Captain Ord pursued the Indians, until approaching the train he occupied the left flank.

Moving forward towards the Spokan river, the Indians still
in front, Lieutenants Ihrie and Howard with Company B, 3d
Artillery, were thrown out on the right flank and instantly cleared the way. And after a continuous fight for seven hours, over
a distance of fourteen miles, we encamped on the banks of
the Spokan river—the troops exhausted by a long and fatiguing march, twenty-five miles without water, and for two-
thirds of the distance under fire. The battle was won, two
chiefs and two brothers of the chief Gearry killed, † besides

---

* The three companies of 3d Artillery above mentioned.
  † Since the battle we learn that Kamiaken, war chief of Yakimas, was nearly killed by
a shell.

many of lesser note either killed or wounded. A kind Providence again protected us; although at many times the balls flew thick and fast through our ranks, yet strange to say, we had but one man slightly wounded.

Again it affords me the highest pleasure to bear witness to the zeal, energy, gallantry and perseverance displayed by the officers and men during this protracted battle.

Brevet Major W. N. Grier, commanding a squadron of 1st Dragoons, composed of his own Company and that of Lieutenant Pender, made a gallant charge at the right moment, killing two and wounding three of the enemy. The Major speaks in the highest terms of the gallantry of Lieutenant Pender, commanding Company "C."

Lieutenant Davidson with Company "E" was rear guard to the general train, and that duty was well performed. Lieutenant Gregg with Company "H" was posted in rear of the howitzer, with a view of making a dash at the enemy, but the ground was so broken that dragoons could not operate effectively.

Captain E. D. Keyes, 3d Artillery, commanding battalion pursuing, was energetic and gallant throughout. Although the troops extended over a mile, yet the Captain was always in the right place at the right time.

Captain Keyes reports the following companies and officers as particularly distinguished.

Company "K," Captain E. O. C. Ord and Lieutenant M. R. Morgan.

Company "G," Captain J. A. Hardie and Lieutenant Ransom.

Company "M," Lieutenants Gibson and Dandy.

Company "A," Lieutenants Tyler and Lyon.

The howitzer battery under Lieutenant White, with detachment of 20 men Company "D," 3d artillery, behaved most gallantly throughout the action. Eight shells were thrown into the midst of the enemy during the fight, and with effect.

The conduct of Lieutenant Kip, Adjutant, of artillery battalion, is noticed by Captain Keyes as having been excellent throughout the day.

The rifle battalion, companies "B" and "E," 9th infantry, under Captain Dent. Captain Dent with his company was on the rear guard to protect the pack train. This duty was handsomely performed, and the train moved along unharmed by the enemy or the fires.

Captain Winder was detached with Lieutenant Fleming and

Company "E" to support the howitzer battery. This service was admirably performed, bravely advancing and pouring in a fire with their rifles when opportunity offered, till the close of the battle.

The friendly Nez Percés were employed chiefly as spies and guides, as well as guards to pack train. As usual they behaved well.

Again I have the pleasure of presenting to the Department the gentlemen of my staff:

1st Lieutenant P. A. Owen, Adjt. 9th Infantry, &c.,

1st Lieutenant J. Mullan, Acting Engineer, &c.,

Captain R. Kirkham, A. Q. M.,

Assistant Surgeon J. F. Hammond, U. S. A.,

Assistant Surgeon J. F. Randolph, U. S. A.

These gentlemen were all on the field, cool, energetic and brave, whether conveying orders to distant points of the line, or attending to their professional duties.

A memoir and topographical sketch of the battle by Lieutenant Mullan, Engineer officer, is herewith enclosed.

Respectfully, &c.,

G. WRIGHT, Col. 9th Inf'y, Com'g.

III.

EXTRACT FROM THE "GENERAL ORDERS."

INDIAN BATTLES FOR THE PAST YEAR AND THE OFFICERS ENGAGED.

GENERAL ORDERS, NO. 22.

Head Quarters of the Army,
New York, Nov. 10, 1858.

The following combats with hostile Indians—in which the conduct of the troops, including volunteers and employés in the United States military service, is deserving of high praise for gallantry and hardships—have occurred, or been brought to the notice of the General-in-Chief, since the publication of General order, No. 14, of 1857, viz:

*　　*　　*　　*　　*　　*　　*

XIV. *September* 1, 1858.—The expedition under Colonel Wright, 9th infantry, composed of companies C, E, H and I, 1st dragoons; A, B, G, K and M, 3d artillery; and B and E, 9th infantry—aggregate five hundred and seventy—with a company of thirty Nez Percés Indians, marched from Fort Walla Walla, Oregon, on the 7th and 15th of August; crossed Snake river on the 25th and 26th; established a post at the crossing, which was left in charge of Brevet Major Wyse and his company D, 3d artillery; and, after a march of nearly a hundred miles, mostly over a forbidding country, during which they were twice attacked, came upon a large body of united Spokan, Cœur d'Alene and Pelouse Indians, of which some four hundred were mounted.

After securing his baggage and supplies, by leaving them under the guard of Company M, 3d artillery, with a mountain howitzer, and a detachment of fifty-four men, commanded by Lieutenants H. G. Gibson, G. B. Dandy and Lyon, the whole under Captain Hardie, 3d artillery, Colonel Wright moved with the rest of his force against the Indians, who had taken possession of a high hill and an adjoining wood, and awaited his attack. They were driven by the foot troops from both their positions into the plain, and then charged and utterly routed by the dragoons, with a loss of some seventeen killed and many wounded.

The troops sustained no loss in either killed or wounded.

Colonel Wright mentions the following as entitled to credit for their coolness and gallantry:

Brevet Major Grier, 1st dragoons; Captain Keyes, 3d artillery; Captain Dent, 9th infantry; 1st Lieutenant Mullan, 2d artillery, acting as topographical engineer and commanding the friendly Nez Percés; 1st Lieutenant P. A. Owen, 9th infantry; Acting Assistant Adjutant General; Captain Kirkham, Assistant Quarter-master; and Assistant Surgeon J. F. Hammond, Medical Department.

The following are also mentioned as having been highly commended by their immediate commanders:

Medical Department.—Assistant Surgeon Randolph.

1st Dragoons.—Lieutenants Davidson, Pender, and 2d Lieutenant Gregg.

1st Sergeant James A. Hall; Sergeants Bernard Korton and Patrick Byrne; Bugler Robert A. Magan, and privates James Kearney and Michael Meara, Company C.

1st Sergeant C. Goetz; Sergeant J. F. Maguire; and Privates J. G. Trimbell, J. Buckley, Wm. Ramage and T. W. Smith, Company E.

1st Sergeant E. Ball; Sergeant M. M. Walker; and Bugler Jacob Muller, Company H.

1st Sergeant W. H. Ingerton; and Sergeant Wm. Davis, Company I.

3rd Artillery.—1st Lieutenants Tyler, White and Ihrie, and 2d Lieutenant Kip.

9th Infantry.—Captain Winder and Lieutenant Fleming.

Nez Percés.—Hute-E-Mah-li-kah, Captain John, Edward and We-ash-kot.

XV. *September 5th to 15th.*—Colonel Wright, 9th Infantry, after defeating the united hostile tribes at the Four Lakes, in Washington Territory, on the 1st (as noticed above, par. XIV.), continued to advance in the Indian country with the same force, and on the 5th of September, was again met by the Spokan, Pelouse and Cœur d'Alene Indians who had been joined by the Pend d'Oreilles.

After a continuous conflict of seven hours, over a distance of fourteen miles, and a fatiguing march, in all, of twenty-five, the Indians were completely routed with the loss of two chiefs —two brothers of the Chief Gearry—and many others of lesser note killed and wounded. The troops had but one man —name not given—wounded, and he but slightly.

Colonel Wright bears witness to the zeal, energy, perseverance and gallantry of his officers and men. He specially mentions the following:

Brevet Major Grier, 1st Dragoons, commanding squadron; Captain Keyes, 3d Artillery, commanding artillery battalion, acting as infantry; Captain Winder and Lieutenant Fleming, 9th Infantry, detached to support the howitzer battery: 1st Lieutenant and Adjutant Owen, 9th Infantry, Acting Assist. Adjutant General; Captain Kirkham, Assistant Quarter-master; Assistant Surgeons J. F. Hammond and J. F. Randolph; and 1st Lieutenant Mullan, 2d Artillery, acting as engineer officer and commanding the friendly Indians.

The following officers are spoken of in the highest terms by their several immediate commanders, viz:

1st Dragoons.—Lieutenant Pender.

3d Artillery.—Company K, Captain E. O. C. Ord and Lieutenant Morgan; Company G, Captain J. A. Hardie and 1st Lieutenant Ransom; Company M, 1st Lieutenant Gibson and 2d Lieutenant Dandy; Company A, 1st Lieutenant Tyler and 2d Lieutenant Lyon.

1st Lieutenant White, commanding howitzer battery—composed of a detachment from Company D, 3d Artillery—and 2d Lieutenant Kip, Adjutant of Keyes' battalion.

Captain Dent, 9th Infantry, with his Company (B), and 1st Lieutenant Davidson, 1st Dragoons, commanding Company E, together with the friendly Nez Percés, guarded the train effectually.

After resting on the 6th, Colonel Wright continued his pursuit of the Indians through their country, arriving at the Cœur d'Alene Mission on the 15th of September. During this march he had a skirmish with the enemy, on the 8th of September, took from them some nine hundred horses, a large number of cattle, with quantities of wheat, oats, roots, &c., &c., all of which were converted to the use of the troops or destroyed.

Those severe blows resulted in the unqualified submission of the Cœur D'Alenes, the dispersion of the other tribes, and, it is not doubted, ere this in the subjugation of the whole alliance.

Results so important, without the loss of a man or animal, gained over tribes brave, well armed, confident in themselves from a recent accidental success, and aided by the many difficulties presented by the country invaded, reflect high credit on all concerned.

Colonel Wright is much to be commended for the zeal, perseverance and gallantry he has exhibited.

To Brigadier General Clarke, commanding the Department of the Pacific, credit is primarily and eminently due for the sound judgment shown in planning and organizing the campaign (including Major Garnett's simultaneous expedition), as well as for his promptness and energy in gathering, from remote points in his extended command, the forces, supplies, &c., necessary for its successful prosecution.

In this merited tribute to the General his staff is included.

     *   *   *   *   *   *   *   *   *   *

By command Brevet Lieutenant General Scott.

L. Thomas, Assistant Adjutant General.

MARY MOSES'S ACCOUNT OF QUALCHIN'S DEATH

*Recorded by William Compton Brown, Colville
Reservation, July 1908, Brown Collection,
Manuscripts, Archives, and Special Collections,
Holland Library, Washington State University,
Pullman, Washington*
Introduced by Clifford E. Trafzer

Sanchow, known to whites and in the literature as Mary Moses, was the daughter of Yakama Chief Owhi and the sister of Qualchin, a prominent Yakama war leader hanged on September 23, 1858, by Col. George Wright. Mary was also the grand-daughter of Weowicht, the patriarch of a prominent Yakama family. She was a member of a powerful family, one of the most important in the Pacific Northwest. She was party to many councils held among her family during the final phases of the Plateau Indian War. Judge William Compton Brown interviewed Mary as part of his research for his book, *The Indian Side of the Story*, which he wrote to provide a Native American voice and perspective of the Indian war of 1855–58. Brown believed that Indians had fought the war as patriots and illustrated his point by interviewing American Indians, including Mary Moses, to illicit their views of historical events.

In 1858, while Colonel Wright and Lieutenant Kip moved north from Fort Walla Walla, Major Robert Garnett traveled from Fort Simcoe in the Yakama country north along the Columbia River. At this time, Mary lived with her father, brothers, and other members of her extended family in the Ellensburg area of Washington.

When Owhi learned of Garnett's command, he moved his people into the Wenatchee Mountains and joined other Indians at the confluence of the Wenatchee and Columbia rivers. According to Mary, her family lost several head of cattle and horses, but they escaped with their lives. Owhi decided to leave the Columbia River and move into the Spokane Country. His small band included his wife, daughter, Mary, and his sons,

Qualchin, Lokout, Leshigh-hite, as well as his daughter, Quomolah, and her husband, Quetalahkin, better known as Chief Moses. The band included some children and remnants of other tribes, but Mary argued that the group was composed primarily of Owhi's family. Although the family sought safety from Garnett in their old camping areas along Spokane River, they ran headlong into Wright's army. In her account, Mary pointed out that contrary to white accounts, Owhi and Qualchin did not lead a large band of warriors in the Spokane Country in order to fight, and they were not seeking a conflict. They were trying to escape the fighting in their own homeland.

Owhi camped at the mouth of the Spokane River where Spokane Indians found his band, reporting that Colonel Wright wanted all Indians to visit his camp to discuss terms of peace. According to Native American accounts, Indians believed that they could enter Wright's camp safely. As a result of Wright's summons, Owhi went to Wright and was soon followed by his son, Qualchin. Mary and the rest of Owhi's family moved south toward Latah Creek and were camped close by when Owhi and Qualchin visited the soldiers. Owhi went into Wright's camp first, and Wright promptly arrested him. Not long afterwards, and acting independently, Qualchin rode into the military camp with Lokout and Qualchin's wife, Whistalks. According to Mary, Chief Moses learned from Spokane Indians that the soldiers had hanged and buried Qualchin. Ten days after his death, Mary and her sisters, Sahmesahpan and Quomolah, reburied their brother not far from present-day Fairfield, Washington.

As for Owhi, Wright planned to hold him hostage but soldiers shot him to death after the chief reportedly attempted an escape. Mary reported that she learned of her father's death from Spokane Indians. When Brown asked Mary if the Indians had ever heard that before his death, Qualchin had condemned Kamiakin, she and other elders denied it, pointing out that the two men were good friends. Unfortunately, Mary's account of the events surrounding Qualchin's death is the best one that has survived. Contemporary Native Americans share oral histories about the hanging of Indians at the end of the war, but the account of Sanchow or Mary Moses is authoritative and accurate, providing a native voice by one who participated in an epic event of Native American history.

Many spellings of Qualchin's name exist in written documents, including that used in this introduction. However, Brown spelled his name Qualchen. Readers of the document below should be aware that Brown uses first person for both himself and for Mary. For this reason, I have italicized Mary's first-person account.

Mary goes on to say that *Owhi went over to Wright's camp by Spokane on account of all these things the Spokane Indians were telling us as coming from Col. Wright, then Moses went over to Wright's camp. Then Qualchen decided to go over and he took his wife and Lo-kout with him. Moses came back to our camp shortly after Qualchen had left but he had missed Qualchen on the way back. The next he* [Moses] *heard from the Spokane Indians* [was] *that Qualchen had been arrested as soon as they got to Wright's camp and that the soldiers had hung Qualchen. Lo-kout soon came back to the camp, with Qualchen's wife. Lo-kout got away through the help of the Spokane Indians who were in Wright's camp. They told the soldiers that Lo-kout was no relation of Qualchen and had just come along with him. No one told Col. Wright who Lo-kout was and he got away and so also did Whistalks, Qualchen's wife. Lo-kout went out into the hills with his folks and hid themselves. Moses went down toward the Moses Coulee country and kept himself concealed for after the soldiers did these things we were all very much afraid. About ten days after Qualchen was hanged, and we were told that the soldiers had left the camp where they were hung Qualchen, my sisters, Quo-mo-lah and Sah-me-sah-pan returned over to the campground the soldiers had just left and found where they the soldiers had buried Qualchen by digging a shallow grave and covering the body with dust, grass, and sticks. Part of the face was exposed and something had chewed the nose off. The soldiers had taken his war bonnet, and all his clothes away. My sisters dug a deeper grave and took up the body and wrapped it in a blanket and put moccasins on the feet and buried it again, and put some shells on the grave.* I have never seen the grave. It is south and west of the city of Spokane, maybe about fifteen miles. *A few days after Qualchen was hung we heard that the soldiers had killed Owhi, whom they had taken along with them.*

We asked Mary specifically if Qualchen had ever received a note from Wright of [Spokane] Garry or anyone. She said no. I explained to her that a report was printed that Qualchen had received a note from someone telling him to go to Wright's camp, but she said there was nothing to it. I asked her if there was any reason to believe that Garry had invited or betrayed Qualchen into Wright's camp. She said no, that they had no such idea in regard to Garry and that she had never heard of such a thing. Her kinsman present also asserted that there was no tradition or belief current amongst the Indians that Garry had betrayed Qualchen. I told her that it was reported that the last words of Qualchen were curses on Kamiaken.

Mary stated that she could not believe that, for *Qualchen and Kamiaken were good friends and that Qualchen and Kamiaken had always helped one another and were good friends to the last.* All the Indians present asserted that they had never heard that Qualchen cursed Kamiaken with his last breath, and all said that there were no Indian traditions to that effect and they could not see how that could have been, as they know of no reason for it.

After we heard that Owhi was killed, my mother and sisters and I made our way back to the Ellensburg Country. It was hard traveling for we were much afraid and only had a few good horses. Our good horses had been stolen by other Indians (called "friendly Indians") and by whites and soldiers. All our land was also taken away from us in the Ellensburg Country and we have never had any land there since. I have two sisters still living in the Ellensburg Country, they are Yan-num-kt and Si-en-wat. They have no land there but still make their homes there. I am going there to visit them now.

V.

KAMIAKIN'S LETTER

October 7, 1855. Dictated to Father Charles M.
Pandosy. From the Click Relander Collection,
Yakima Valley Regional Library,
Yakima, Washington
Introduced by Clifford E. Trafzer

The Walla Walla Council of 1855 created the Yakama, Umatilla, and Nez Perce treaties and reservations. It also created much hostility among many Native Americans of the Columbia Plateau against the United States. Chief Kamiakin, a Yakama and Palouse chief, rallied many diverse Indians against the Americans. Not long after war between the tribes and Americans began, Kamiakin asked his friend and neighbor at Ahtanum Creek, Oblate Father Charles M. Pandosy, of the St. Joseph Mission, to compose a letter to the Americans. The letter appears below in its entirety.

Kamiakin's letter reveals the chief's belief that Governor Isaac Stevens caused the war because of his words and message at the Walla Walla Council among the Cayuses. Stevens proposed to relocate fourteen different tribes and bands onto the Yakama Reservation, forcing the Indians into a defensive war. Kamiakin was disturbed that Stevens planned to place tribes speaking three distinct language families—Sahaptin, Salish, and Chinook—onto a single land base because many of them disliked each other, which would cause greater conflict. The chief felt that whites had perpetuated several murders against Indians, but not one white killer had been hanged for their crimes. He believed that whites had treated Indians like dogs and had insulted native people by claiming that their wealth in cattle and horses was the result of white contact, not hard work by native people. More than once in his letter, Kamiakin mentions that American policies of concentration of the native population would result in food shortages and famine.

Kamiakin blamed the Yakama War of 1855 on Stevens and the Americans who wanted to steal Indian lands for the benefit of whites. This had been the position of Native Americans since 1492, and it was one Kamiakin shared with American Indians from the Atlantic Seaboard to the Pacific Ocean. Kamiakin argued that the immediate cause of the war was the killing of Agent Andrew Jackson Bolon by Mosheel and Wahpiwahpilah. Kamiakin states that these Yakamas murdered Bolon because the white man threatened to send troops from Fort Dalles to destroy the tribes. Thus, the Yakamas killed Bolon as a defensive measure.

The native leader offered the Americans an olive branch at the end of his letter, asking the soldiers to consider his words and negotiate in a friendly manner. However, if the Americans chose war, Kamiakin threatened to rally 10,000 warriors in a confederacy, a promise Kamiakin could not have fulfilled. Kamiakin noted that he would not allow native women and children to fall into the hands of Americans who would sexually abuse and enslave them. Instead he would order his men to kill them. Kamiakin suggests that the Indians had been willing to allow whites to settle in the Inland Northwest, but Kamiakin himself had stood firm against white settlement because of his knowledge of whites in eastern Oregon and Washington as well as northern California.

After some initial Indian victories against American troops in 1855, the tribes lost ground. In October and November 1855, Major Gabriel Rains and Colonel James Nesmith set out to "exterminate" the tribes. With over five hundred troops, the soldiers marched through the Yakama Country on their way to Kamiakin's village. The chief and his people had retreated north with Father Pandosy. Before burning the St. Joseph Mission to the ground, Rains found Kamiakin's letter but ignored the offer of peace. In a response to the letter, Rains wrote that Indians had caused the war and that whites were "thirsting" for Indian blood and planned to feed the hungry crows with the bodies of dead Indians. He promised no peace, only literal extermination of native men, women, and children. Kamiakin's words that elicited such a lurid response are presented below and are offered as one of the most important and revealing documents. It provides an Indian voice during the tragic drama of the Yakama War:

After a conversation that Father Pandosy had made on the results of war and advantages of peace, the savages said to F. Pandosy.

"Write to the soldiers, tell them that we are quiet, friend to American, that we were not thinking of war at all; but the way in which the governor has talked to us at the Cayuses at the Walla Walla Council has irritated us and made us determine to general war which will end with complete destruction of all the savages [this is Pandosy's usage for Native Americans, common for the time period] or all Americans.

"If the governor had told us, my children, I am asking you [for] a piece of land in each tribe for the Americans, but the land and your country is still yours, we would have given willingly what he would have asked us and we would have lived with all others as brothers. But he has taken us in number and thrown us out of our native country in a strange land among a people who is our enemy, for between us we are enemy, in a place where its people do not even have enough to eat for themselves. [Kamiakin is referring to concentrating 14 diverse tribes onto a single land base and calling it the Yakama Reservation.]

"Then we have said, now we know perfectly the heart of the Americans; since a long time. They have hanged us without knowing if we are right or wrong; but they [Native Americans] have never killed or hanged one American, though there is no place where an American has not killed savages. We are therefore dogs. They tell us that our ancestors had no horses or cattle, nor crops nor instruments to garden, that we have received everything of these riches from the Americans; that the country was already full of us and at the same time they chase us from our native lands, as if they were telling us: I have sent you all these things so that you [can] increase them until I send my people [to] arrive, as soon as they will be on the place they will find what to eat. You want, therefore you Americans, [to] make us die of famine little by little. It is better for us to die at once. It is you, governor, who has wanted war, by these words: the country will be for us from all tribes, all nations you will go to such place [the reservation] and leave here your land. Our heart has been torn when you have said these words. You have shot the first gun. Our heart has been broken. There is only one breath left; we did not have the strength to answer. Then we took common cause with our enemy to defend all together our nationality and our country.

"However the war was not going to start too soon, but the Americans who were going to the mines having shot some savages because they did not want to give them their wives [miners going to the Colville mines raped native women], we have taken the care of defending ourselves. Then came Mr. Bolon who has strongly insulted us, threatened us of war, death when announcing [to] us that he was going back to The Dalles from where he would send soldiers to destroy us. Nevertheless we have left him pass quietly, after having thought of what he had just told us, we went to join him. We were without arms and without any idea to kill him but as he went on talking to us with too much harshness and threatened us with soldiers, we have seized him and have killed him so that we can say it is not us who have started a war, but we have only defended ourselves.

"If the soldiers and the Americans [settlers] after having read the letter and taken knowledge of the motives which bring us to fight, want to retire or treat [us in a] friendly [manner], we will consent to put [our] arms down and to grant you a piece of land in every tribe [as long as you] do not force us to be exiled from our native country, otherwise we are decided to be cut to pieces and if we lose, the men who keep the camp in which are the wives and children will kill them rather than see them fall into the hands of the Americans to make them their toys. For we have heart and respect ourselves. Write this to the soldiers and the Americans and they [may] give you an answer to know what they think. If they do not answer it is because they want war; we will then [get] 1050 men assembled.

"Some only will go to battle, but as soon as the war is started the news will spread along all our nations and in a few days we will be more than 10,000. If peace is wanted, we will consent to it, but it must be written to us so we may know about it."

INDEX